The **FLAGS** of
CIVIL WAR NORTH CAROLINA

THE THREE COLONELS

Lt. Col. John R. Lane, Col. Henry K. Burgwyn, Jr., and Col. Zebulon B. Vance all led the 26th North Carolina Regiment at different times during the war.

The FLAGS of CIVIL WAR NORTH CAROLINA

by Glenn Dedmondt

PELICAN PUBLISHING COMPANY
Gretna 2003

*The word "Pelican" and the depiction of a pelican are trademarks
of Pelican Publishing Company, Inc., and are registered in the
U.S. Patent and Trademark Office.*

Library of Congress Cataloging-in-Publication Data

Dedmondt, Glenn.
  The flags of Civil War North Carolina / by Glenn Dedmondt.
    p. cm.
Includes bibliographical references and index.
  ISBN 1-56554-992-9 (pbk. : alk. paper)
  1. North Carolina—History—Civil War, 1861-1865—Flags. 2. North
Carolina—History—Civil War, 1861-1865—Regimental histories. 3.
Flags—North Carolina. 4. United States—History—Civil War,
1861-1865—Flags. 5. United States—History—Civil War,
1861-1865—Regimental histories. I. Title.
  E573.4 .D42 2003
  929.9'2'0975609034—dc21

                2002011378

Printed in China

Published by Pelican Publishing Company, Inc.
1000 Burmaster Street, Gretna, Louisiana 70053

Respectfully dedicated
to the memory of

Zebulon Baird Vance

Congressman, Soldier, Governor

In North Carolina we have had great men, any one of whom was and is an honor to the State, and of whom our people have been and still are justly proud of; but it is no disparagement to those to say that Zebulon Baird Vance was the Mount Mitchell of all our great men, and that in the affections and love of the people he towered above them all. As ages to come will not be able to mar the grandeur and greatness of Mount Mitchell, so they will not be able to efface from the hearts and minds of the people the name and memory of their beloved Vance.

Senator Thomas J. Jarvis

Contents

IV. The Naval Flags

Preface

At our parties' political conventions, each state announces its decision with much fanfare, usually something to the tune of "Mr. Chairman, the *great* and *sovereign* state of (fill in the state) chooses to cast its (fill in the number) votes for the great and honorable (fill in the name)."

Although it makes for amusing and raucous media coverage, the delegates surely must understand the ludicrousness in the use of the adjective *sovereign*. At this point in our republic, state sovereignty is a state of mind, relegated to rambunctious conventions and history books. It was not always so.

One of my favorite photographs shows the boys of the Tarheel State being welcomed home from World War I. What a happy crowd! The citizens are there, the doughboys are there, and the Capitol is colorfully and elaborately decorated. Along the first level of the stately old marble structure are the flags of Great Britain, North Carolina, France, and Italy.

One distinction occurs in the display of these flags of state. North Carolina's is elevated a full *five feet* above the rest. At the second level is a "Welcome Back" banner to the Pershing Crusaders, "The Flower of Carolina." The largest flag shown, a rectangular Confederate battle flag, is hanging centered on the portico, flanked by two red, white, and blue patriotic buntings. On the outside of the upper level are two slightly smaller U.S. national flags. Atop the dome, framed against the Tarheel-blue sky and dancing in the Southern breeze, is the red, white, and blue lone-star flag of the *sovereign* state of North Carolina. This was 1919.

Few people have ever understood the word *sovereignty* as have North Carolinians. Perhaps this concept of self-rule was born in the days of the Lords Proprietors when the king had relinquished his authority over the colony and the Proprietors chose not to exert theirs. The concept was certainly put to the test in the days of the revolution when the state, along with her sister states in America, waged war for their independence from the tyranny of monarchy.

The constitution through which this war was waged, the Articles of Confederation, bound the American states together in a loosely knit alliance and unreservedly assured and protected the sovereignty of the individual states. *Sovereignty* does not come cheaply. North Carolina's free and independent status was demanded and earned only through strength of will and purpose.

The state's sovereignty was announced to the world in the 1783 Treaty of

Welcome home

Paris when "His Britannic Majesty" sued for peace with the United States, addressing each of the thirteen states by name and status as "free, *sovereign, and independent states.*"

When North Carolina's sovereignty was threatened by the proposal of a new constitution delegating broader authority to a central Federal government, the Old North State balked. Wary of a constitution that seemed to be a threat to personal liberty and state sovereignty, North Carolina declined to enter the pact. Threats and cajoling from neighbor states did not deter North Carolina from its course; it would not sacrifice its newly won independent, sovereign status on the altar of unity.

Though beat upon by waves of detractors who accused North Carolina of "destructive purposes" and "disharmony," the state held true to its principles. For fourteen months, North Carolina was a singular republic among the world's states. Only with the inclusion of a Bill of Rights, particularly the 10th amendment assuring "states' rights," did North Carolina sign the contract.

It was a fitful contract. Almost immediately, the union was adrift when the New England states threatened secession in protest of the War of 1812, a war in which North Carolina supported the country and defended its own shores. The union was threatened during the Tariff Debates, which culminated in South Carolina's Ordinance of Nullification. Civil war was narrowly averted with a tariff compromise in Congress. Through the arguments, compromises, pontification, and gavel rapping of the 1830s, 1840s, and 1850s, North Carolina remained steadfast in its quest for union *and* sovereignty, an uneasy balancing act.

For many states the balance seemed overly precarious, and with the election of Abraham Lincoln, a pro-tariff ex-Whig, South Carolina left the union of states. Although secession fever had caught on to some degree in North Carolina, for the most part the Old North State stayed true to the rock of union *and* sovereignty. On January 9, 1861, a Federal ship invaded Charleston harbor and was driven back. While the rest of the South followed South Carolina's lead in secession, North Carolina remained true to the Union, not out of unabashed love for the Union but from an assured position that the state's sovereignty had not been compromised.

By April, all eyes were on Charleston, South Carolina. For four months a Federal garrison had occupied Fort Sumter. As Confederate peace commissioners in Washington, D.C., begged an audience with the new president, Lincoln was driving events that would give him an opportunity to forge a new Union.

When announcements of a new supply mission to Fort Sumter were received in Charleston, Gen. P. G. T. Beauregard was given orders to drive the

Federal garrison from the fort. On April 12, 1861, a cannon bombardment began that ended with the fort's surrender on April 14. The United States president called for troops to put down the "insurrection" in South Carolina. North Carolina was ordered to furnish two regiments of militia for immediate service. The balance of union and sovereignty was broken.

Gov. John Willis Ellis of North Carolina, a mild-mannered Unionist, will forever live in history for his fiery reply to the illegal request:

"Your dispatch is received, and if genuine, which its extraordinary character leads me to doubt, I have to say in reply, that I regard the levy of troops by the administration for the purpose of subjugating the states of the South, as a violation of the Constitution, and as a gross usurpation of power. I can be no party to this wicked violation of the laws of the country and to this war upon the liberties of a free people. You can get no troops from North Carolina."

John W. Ellis

On April 17, 1861, Governor Ellis wrote his famous "Proclamation" in which he decried Lincoln's call for troops as a *"high-handed act of tyrannical outrage . . . in violation of all constitutional law, in utter disregard of every sentiment of humanity and Christian civilization, and conceived in a spirit of aggression unparalleled by any act of recorded history."*

He called a special session of the North Carolina legislature to begin on May 1, 1861, and exhorted all *"good citizens throughout the State to be mindful that their first allegiance is due to the Sovereignty which protects their homes and dearest interests, as their first service is due for the sacred defence of their hearths, and of the soil which holds the graves of our glorious dead.*

"United action in defence of the sovereignty of North Carolina, and of the rights of the South, becomes now the duty of all."

The gauntlet was thrown. There would be no turning back, and on May 20, 1861, the sovereign state of North Carolina left the Union of States formed by their grandfathers.

Sovereignty demands a symbol, and on that same day a committee was formed to design and produce a flag for North Carolina. The product of this committee was the beautiful lone-star sovereignty flag so familiar to North Carolinians today. Every Tarheel regiment outfitted for the war would bear with them a flag of this design, a reminder of their duty in the *"defence of their hearths and of the soil which holds the graves of our glorious dead."*

It would not be John Ellis' fate to guide his state in the fight for sovereignty. On July 7, 1861, this brave leader died. A special election was held and another former Unionist, Zebulon Baird Vance, was elected.

Vance remembered the day he heard of Lincoln's call for volunteers:

"The Union men had every prop knocked out from under them, and . . . were plunged into the secession movement.

"For myself, I will say that I was canvassing for the Union with all my strength; I was addressing a large and excited crowd, large numbers of whom were armed, and literally had my hand extended upward in pleading for peace and the Union of our Fathers, when the telegraphic news was announced of the firing on Fort Sumter and the President's call for 75,000 volunteers.

"When my hand came down from that impassioned gesticulation, it fell slowly and sadly by the side of a Secessionist. I immediately, with altered voice and manner, called upon the assembled multitude to volunteer not to fight against but for South Carolina. I said, if war must come, I prefer to be with my own people. If we had to shed blood I preferred to shed Northern rather than Southern blood. If we had to slay I had rather slay strangers than my own kindred and neighbors; and that it was better, whether right or wrong, that communities and states should get together and face the horrors of war in a body—sharing a common fate, rather than endure the unspeakable calamities of internecine strife."

But if anyone mistakes these words as indecisive or noncommittal, they could not be farther from the truth. Under the leadership of Gov. Zebulon Vance, North Carolina waged a struggle for its right to be with a determined tenacity unparalleled in history. North Carolina furnished for the Southern cause 125,000 men, more than its voting population. One-fifth of the Confederate losses in the Seven Days battle, one-third at Fredericksburg and Chancellorsville, and one-fourth at Gettysburg were North Carolinians. Of the twenty-seven regiments suffering the highest casualties at Gettysburg, thirteen were from North Carolina. In the entire war, 19,673 North Carolinians were killed in battle—more than one-fourth of the total Confederate battle deaths—and 20,602 died of disease, a total loss of 40,275, more than any other Confederate state.

"Well and truly," said Zebulon Vance,

"North Carolina performed her duty as the result on many a stricken field will show. First and last she sent to the armies of the Confederacy not relatively but absolutely more soldiers than any other state in the South, furnished more supplies, equipped her troops better . . . there was not a sacrifice she was called upon to make for the good of the Southern cause that she did not make and make cheerfully."

The cause of State Sovereignty was forcibly suppressed with the end of the War for Southern Independence. The flame that burned so brightly in 1863 has dimmed to a flicker with the passing of time. The shout that echoed across the land has diminished to a whisper. Once the topic of conversation in every Southern parlor, State Sovereignty now is barely mentioned in U.S. history classes.

But the lone-star flags that heralded the rebirth of a state, the flags that announced to the world that North Carolina would fight for her right to exist, the flags that were carried with the gallants who marched off in the *"sacred defence of their hearths,"* still live. Though battered and torn, they still speak of a day when boys in gray stood with their faces to the foe and their backs to their homes in defiance of tyranny. Let the flags speak.

"God Bless Gallant Old North Carolina."

Gen. Robert E. Lee

Introduction

North Carolina's flags during the War Between the States can be classified into four main groups: company flags, state flags, national flags, and battle flags.

Company Flags: North Carolina's oldest state symbol is the Great Seal of State, although it has been changed considerably since the adoption of the first seal by the Proprietors in 1663. By the 1850s, the Seal of North Carolina had been in use for some time and is quite similar to the modern-day seal. In 1860, the official seal depicted the figures of "Liberty and Plenty," looking toward each other. Liberty, with a rod in her hand on which is the cap of Liberty, has in her other hand a scroll with the word "CONSTITUTION." Plenty is bearing "three heads of grain" in one hand and with the other is supporting the horn of plenty.

The background usually depicts North Carolina's geography from the mountains to the sea. This Great Seal, with minor variations, was the central device in most of North Carolina's flags before, during, and just after secession. These flags tend to be as original as the individuals who handcrafted them for the new companies of the State. From the exquisitely hand-painted company flag of the Guilford Greys to the hastily constructed 1st National variant of the Enfield Blues, these flags are a distinctive and varied group of symbols representing a diverse group of Tarheels who rushed from their homes to defend their state.

State Flags: On May 20, 1861, the day that the secession resolution was adopted by the state of North Carolina, an ordinance to adopt a state flag was presented by Col. John D. Whitford. A committee of seven was formed, with Colonel Whitford appointed chairman. The original ordinance stated that "the flag of this State shall be a blue field with a white V thereon, and a star, encircling which shall be the words, 'Sirgit Astrum, May 20, 1775.'"

This first proposal from Whitford's committee would never become a reality. Fortunately, the colonel and his committee consulted an artist from Raleigh, William Jarl Browne, for advice. Browne prepared a model for a state flag and submitted it to the committee for approval.

The "Browne" flag was not at all like that described in the original proposal. Browne's flag was obviously based on the flag of the Republic of Texas, the "Lone Star State," with colors slightly rearranged. The field along the hoist would be red, centered with a five-pointed star encircled by two dates, May 20, 1775, and May 20, 1861, the date of North Carolina's secession. Two horizontal bars, blue over white, would make up the remainder of the field.

The following ordinance was approved by the North Carolina Convention on June 22, 1861:

An Ordinance in Relation to a State Flag

"Be it ordained by this Convention, and it is hereby ordained by the authority of the same, That the Flag of North Carolina shall consist of a red field with a white star in the center, and with the inscription, above the star, in a semi-circular form, of 'May 20th, 1775,' and below the star, in a semi-circular form, of 'May 20th, 1861.' That there shall be two bars of equal width, and the length of the field shall be equal to the bar, the width of the field being equal to both bars: the first bar shall be blue, and second shall be white: and the length of the flag shall be one-third more than its width."

The first manufacture of these new flags was commissioned by Quartermaster-General Lawrence O'Brian Branch. In August 1861, he ordered flags to be made for the first ten regiments of North Carolina State Troops. These flags were procured through an agent in Virginia from J. W. Belote of Norfolk at a cost of $50 per flag.

Later Branch ordered one more silk flag for the 1st Regiment North Carolina Volunteers, the "Bethel Regiment." These first silk flags, with their scrolls and gold borders, were far more elaborate than the State Ordinance required. Subsequent flags, made from bunting, would be more in line with the ordinance and were apparently issued to each North Carolina regiment at its formation.

National Flags: The regiments of North Carolina carried Confederate colors as well as State colors. Often these colors were based on the three national flags of the Confederate States of America.

1st National: This flag, adopted by an order of the Flag Committee, March 4, 1861, is today known as the "Stars and Bars." With its blue canton, and field of alternating red/white/red, this flag saw service over government buildings as well as in the field. North Carolina flags of this service were carried by the 2nd Regiment, Yadkin Gray Eagles, Forsythe Rifles, Rutherford Volunteers, and the 33rd and 34th Regiments.

2nd National: This flag, approved by the Confederate Congress, May 1, 1863, is also known as the "Stainless Banner." It consisted of a field of white with a canton in the pattern of the square battle flag. This national flag also saw service in the field. Some notable examples of North Carolina units using the 2nd National flag are the 13th, 17th, 42nd, and 72nd Regiments.

3rd National: On March 4, 1865, the Confederate Congress changed the pattern of the national flag by adding a red border to the fly end of the 2nd National. The only known example of this flag in use by North Carolina units is the Sugar Loaf flag, used in the Wilmington campaigns of 1865.

Battle Flags: North Carolina regiments that saw service in the Army of Northern Virginia were issued flags from the Richmond Depot. The design of this square battle flag, changed slightly over eight issues, is the pattern so familiar to students of Confederate history.

1st (silk) issue: First created by Richmond sewing circles, this flag was issued to units around Richmond in November 1861. These were 48" square, with 8"-wide blue bars displaying only twelve stars and bordered with 2"-wide gold edging. Because of the shortage of red silk, the field of these flags tended toward rose or pink.

1st (bunting) issue: These 48" square flags kept the same configuration as the silk issue, except that the material was wool bunting, the borders were orange, and a thirteenth star was added.

2nd (bunting) issue: In this issue of June 1862, the width of the blue bar was decreased to 5". For these first three mentioned issues, battle honors were allowed and sometimes specified for honorable regimental participation in battles. These first battle honors were imprinted to cotton patches and sewn to the flag. One example is the 2nd issue flag of the 4th Regiment.

3rd (bunting) issue: This largest issue of square battle flags began in July 1862 and continued through the spring of 1864. The dimensions were the same as the 2nd bunting issue but the borders were changed to white. Battle honors were applied to these flags with paint. In some earlier distributions, scalloped block letters were applied in white, one example being that of the

37th Regiment. Later, 3rd issue flags displayed blue block letters.

4th (bunting) issue: This issue of 51" square flags began in May 1864 and had blue bars approximately 7" wide. Previous flags had stars approximately 6" apart. In the 4th issue, star spacing was increased to 8".

5th (bunting) issue: This flag, first issued in autumn 1864, was slightly rectangular, 48" x 50". The width of the cross was decreased to 5" with star intervals of 9".

6th (bunting) issue: In these 48" square flags the star interval was decreased to 8".

7th (bunting) issue: The star interval was decreased to 7" on a 5"-wide blue cross.

As a few North Carolina units saw service in the western theater of the war, they were issued flags representative of their western commands. One such flag is the Department of Alabama and Mississippi battle flag issued to the 39th Regiment North Carolina State Troops, whose gallant service took them to Murfreesboro, Tennessee; Jackson, Mississippi; and Chickamauga, Georgia.

Because of North Carolina's distinctive method of unit designation (see Appendix I), the flags in this book are shown in order of North Carolina State Troop designation. For instance, the flags of the 1st North Carolina Cavalry will be found listed as 9th Regiment North Carolina State Troops; the flags of the 1st North Carolina Artillery will be found listed as 10th Regiment North Carolina State Troops.

The collection of illustrations and histories begins with **The Leaders.** Governor Ellis' flag is the only flag associated with a political leader, the others being headquarters flags of general-grade officers. These are followed by **Garrison Flags** and then with a group of **Unidentified Flags.** The largest section is **North Carolina Regiments.** In this section are shown the company and regimental flags of North Carolina's fighting men. These are listed in regimental numerical order as mentioned earlier. The last section, **Naval Flags,** illustrates a small portion of North Carolina's war along the Atlantic coast.

A degree of artistic license has been used in illustrating these flags. Because of the similar construction and design of the regimental battle flags, most have been illustrated with their battle damage shown. Some, in which the damage was minimal and does not reflect an individual wear pattern, have been shown intact.

A few flags that began as works of art suffered greatly in the field. Because of the artistry of the original flags, I have tried to show these as they were when new. All of these flags must be actually seen to be truly appreciated. Even the flags classified as in "good condition" are fragile to the touch. The ones listed as "fragile" or "shattered" are so deteriorated they cannot even be touched safely. These are in desperate need of preservation.

By far the largest collection is at the Museum of History in Raleigh, but a large number are protected at the Museum of the Confederacy in Richmond, Virginia. Both museums have an active flag conservation program, and contributions from interested parties are always welcome.

It is my hope that through this work, North Carolinians may become more aware of their rich Southern heritage, the role of these flags in freedom's struggle, and the tangible legacy of these banners representing the dreams of their forefathers.

Gov. John W. Ellis

John Ellis was born in Rowan County and was a graduate of the University of North Carolina. He was governor of North Carolina from 1859 to 1861. During his term of office, while other Southern states were leaving the Union, he led the state of North Carolina in an attempt to remain neutral. However, when U.S. president Abraham Lincoln demanded 75,000 troops to "put down the rebellion," Governor Ellis bristled. He wrote his famous reply in defense of North Carolina's sovereignty, stating, "You can get no troops from North Carolina." He called for a special session of the state legislature, and on May 20, 1860, North Carolina tied her future to the newly formed Confederacy.

Governor Ellis died shortly afterward on July 7, 1861. He is buried in the Old English Cemetery in Salisbury.

This flag was made by the ladies of St. Mary's School, in Raleigh, and presented to the governor before his death. It is 42" (hoist) x 63" (fly). The red field is 23" wide, while the royal blue and white bars are 21" wide. Red twill tape, ¼" wide, is wrapped as reinforcement to three edges. The white satin star is 10½" in diameter. The letters and numerals are of white satin and sewn to the red field. The uppercase letters are 3¼" high, the numerals are 3" high, and the superscripts are 1½" high.

Museum of the Confederacy, Richmond, Va.

Brig. Gen. Lawrence O'Brian Branch
Headquarters Flag

Lawrence O'Brian Branch enlisted as a private in the Raleigh Rifles in April 1861. The experience this 41-year-old son of North Carolina brought would take him quickly to positions of leadership. He was born in 1820 in Halifax, North Carolina, taken by his parents to Tennessee, and orphaned at the age of seven. He was brought back to North Carolina by his uncle and guardian, Gov. John Branch.

When Governor Branch was appointed Secretary of the Navy in 1829, Lawrence went with him to Washington, where he studied under Salmon P. Chase. He graduated with first honors from Princeton at the age of 18.

He resided for a while in Florida and participated in the Seminole War. Returning to his home state, he became president of the Raleigh & Gaston Railroad and in 1855 was elected to Congress. After the invasion of Charleston harbor on January 9, 1861, Branch became an ardent secessionist.

He did not remain a private long. On May 20, the date of North Carolina's secession, he accepted the office of state quartermaster-general. In this capacity, he was instrumental in issuing the first North Carolina flags to State

Troops. On June 22, 1861, an ordinance was written establishing the pattern of a new state flag, and in August, Branch, in his role as quartermaster-general, ordered the purchase of ten silk flags. These were issued to the first ten regiments of State Troops.

Resigning his office for field service, he was elected colonel of the 33rd Regiment. In January 1862, he was promoted to brigadier general. His brigade consisted of the 7th, 18th, 28th, 33rd, and 37th Regiments. He led his brigade at New Berne, Mechanicsville, Cold Harbor, Frayser's Farm, and Malvern Hill, earning fame for his courage and coolness in battle. He led his men through Cedar Run, 2nd Manassas, Fairfax Court House, and Harpers Ferry.

From Harpers Ferry, Branch's brigade, as a part of A. P. Hill's famous division, rushed to the aid of General Lee at Sharpsburg, arriving in time to drive Burnside's Corps from the field. Soon after this success, a group of officers, Branch included, were consulting with General Hill when a sharpshooter's bullet struck the gallant North Carolinian in the head, killing him instantly.

Of Lawrence O'B. Branch, General Hill said, "The Confederacy has to mourn the loss of a gallant soldier and accomplished gentleman. He was my senior brigadier, and one to whom I could have intrusted the command of the division, with all confidence."

General Branch's Headquarters flag was of the Confederate 1st National pattern. The flag is missing considerable material but was probably 48" (hoist) x 72" (fly) when new. The blue canton is 32" square and displays twelve 5" diameter stars. These stars, with slightly rounded rays, are a feature of the flag of the 33rd North Carolina State Troops, and it is likely that each regiment of Branch's Brigade was issued a similar flag. The circle of stars has within it the embroidered inscription "Gen. L. O'B. Branch/1862/N.C." in script letters.

North Carolina Museum of History, Raleigh, N.C.

Maj. Gen. Robert F. Hoke
Headquarters Flag

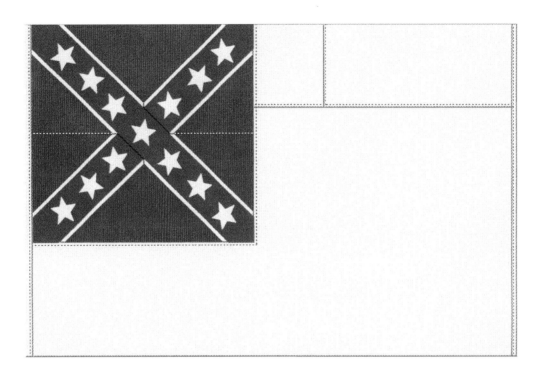

Robert F. Hoke was born in Lincolnton, North Carolina, on May 27, 1837, and educated at the Kentucky Military Institute. He entered the military service of the state in April 1861, as a member of Company K, 1st Regiment Volunteers. He was immediately commissioned as a 2nd lieutenant, and as captain was commended for "coolness, judgment and efficiency" in D. H. Hill's report of the battle of Big Bethel. In September, he became major of the 1st Regiment.

At the reorganization, he was commissioned lieutenant colonel of the 33rd Regiment. He commanded five companies at New Berne, on March 14, 1862, and was distinguished for gallantry. When the colonel was captured at New Berne, Hoke was given command of the regiment and, as a part of Branch's Brigade, led them in the Virginia battles of Hanover Court House, Mechanicsville, Gaines' Mill, Frayser's Farm, and Malvern Hill.

After promotion to colonel, Hoke led the regiment at 2nd Manassas and Sharpsburg. On Colonel Avery's return, Hoke was given command of the 21st Regiment North Carolina State Troops. He led this regiment through the battle of Fredericksburg, where he earned the praises of both Generals Early and Jackson.

In January 1863, Hoke was promoted to brigadier general and given command of Trimble's Brigade, composed of the 6th, 21st, 54th, and 57th North Carolina Regiments and the 1st North Carolina Battalion. During the battle of Chancellorsville, he was severely wounded. This wound prevented his participation in the Pennsylvania campaign.

Recovering from his injuries, he reported back for duty. His brigade was sent to North Carolina, where it fought in the attempt to retake New Berne.

On April 17, 1864, Hoke's Brigade attacked the Federal forts at Plymouth, North Carolina, vigorously pushing assaults while the *C.S.S. Albemarle* attacked the coastal batteries and ships from the river. Due to the tremendous success of this operation, Hoke was promoted to major general, the commission bearing the date of his victory.

As the situation became more tenuous in Virginia, Hoke was sent to join General Beauregard, and on May 10 was given command of six brigades and sent to Drewry's Bluff. His conduct of this fight was superb. One of his brigades, Hagood's, captured five pieces of artillery. At Cold Harbor he held one of the most important parts of the line with his division, repelling furious assaults, and fought in the June battles at Petersburg.

In December 1864, he was moved with his division to Wilmington to confront Butler's attack on Fort Fisher. He foiled the first attack on the fort. In the second assault, Hoke advanced two brigades and drove in the enemy's pickets. Unfortunately, General Bragg, fearful of an enemy attack on Wilmington, called back Hoke's forces. Fort Fisher was lost.

At the battle of Bentonville, Hoke's division consistently repelled the advances of Sherman's army. With extreme bravery and presence of mind, Hoke turned disaster into victory at each point he met the enemy, earning the praises of General Hampton, who said, "Bragg, by reason of his rank, was in command of this division, but it was really Hoke's division, and Hoke directed the fighting."

On May 1, 1865, after the surrender of General Johnston's Army of Tennessee at Durham, General Hoke issued a farewell address to his division, in which he said:

"You are paroled prisoners, not slaves. The love of liberty which led you into the contest burns as brightly in your hearts as ever. Cherish it. Associate it with the history of your past. Transmit it to your children. Teach them the rights of freemen and teach them to maintain them. Teach them the proudest day in all your proud career was that on which you enlisted as Southern soldiers."

Maj. Gen. Robert F. Hoke's headquarters flag is a 2nd National. It is 47" (hoist) x 70" (fly). The canton is 31" (hoist) x 34" (fly). The red field of the canton is crossed with 5"-wide blue bars forming a St. Andrew's cross, which is edged with ½" white cotton fimbriation. Thirteen white cotton stars, 4⅞"-5" point to point, are sewn to the cross.

North Carolina Museum of History, Raleigh, N.C.

Brig. Gen. Rufus Barringer
Headquarters Flag

Rufus Barringer was born in Cabarrus County, North Carolina, in 1821. He graduated from North Carolina University in 1842, studied law, and settled in Concord. He served in both the State House and Senate and was outspoken in his support of the Union. However, when secession seemed imminent, he advocated the arming of the state and was among the first to volunteer. From Concord, he raised a company of cavalry, of which he was chosen captain, his commission dating from May 16, 1861.

This company became Company F, 1st Regiment North Carolina Cavalry. In August, he was promoted to major and three months later to lieutenant colonel. In June 1864, he was promoted to brigadier general and assumed command of the 1st N.C. Cavalry Brigade, consisting of the 1st, 2nd, 3rd, and 5th Regiments.

General Barringer was in seventy-six actions and was wounded three times, the most severe being at Brandy Station. He had two horses shot from under him at other engagements. He led troops in battle at Willis' Church, Brandy Station, Auburn Mills, Buckland Races, where he led the charge, Davis' Farm, where he was commander; and he was in command of a division at Reams' Station.

His brigade was distinguished at Chamberlain Run on March 31, 1865, when it forded a deep stream one hundred yards wide, saddle-girth deep, under a galling fire, and drove back a division of Federal cavalry. On April 3, 1865, at Namozine Church, he was taken prisoner by a party of "Jesse Scouts" from Sheridan's command disguised as Confederates. With his fellow officers, General Ewell included, Barringer was sent to City Point.

It was also at this time that the general's headquarters flag was captured by William H. Woodall, one of the scouts. The flag is 47" (hoist) x 48½" (fly). The red field is crossed with 5"-wide blue bars forming a St. Andrew's cross. The bars are edged with ½" white cotton fimbriation. Thirteen 3¾"-3⅞" white cotton stars are evenly spaced on the cross. After its capture, the flag was given the War Department number 320.

After the war, Barringer resided in Charlotte and practiced law. He became a Republican and ran for political office. He wrote and attended United Confederate Veterans meetings. He worked tirelessly on behalf of his state, church, and former comrades. His son Paul was by his side at the time of his death. One of the general's last injunctions to his son was: "Remember Company F; see that not one of them ever suffers from want. They ever loved me, they were ever faithful to me, and Paul, always stand by our Confederate soldiers, and North Carolina. Let her never be traduced."

General Barringer died February 3, 1895.

North Carolina Museum of History, Raleigh, N.C.

Maj. Gen. Bryan Grimes
Headquarters Flag

At the battle of Seven Pines, Lt. Col. Bryan Grimes led the 4th Regiment North Carolina State Troops in a charge on the enemy. During the fight, his horse's head was blown off by enemy artillery. The poor animal fell dead, pinning the officer, who, even in his captive state, waved his sword and shouted, "Forward!" to his men, encouraging them onward. Extricated from his painful position, he seized the regimental flag and personally led his men in their successful charge.

Such stories of bravery and gallantry, so rare in the study of military history, are commonplace in the study of Bryan Grimes. Throughout the war, a total of seven horses would die beneath this brave man. When his superiors were disabled, he quickly stepped to the front. When sick and injured, he continued leading his men, fighting through his pain. After Mechanicsville, General Anderson said, "Colonel Grimes and his regiment are the keystone of my brigade."

At Chancellorsville, he and his regiment were distinguished on all three days of battle, on the third driving the enemy from their breastworks at the point of the bayonet. In this fight, Grimes narrowly escaped death. He and his regiment were the first to enter Gettysburg, driving the enemy before them. When General Ramseur was wounded at Spottsylvania, Grimes took command of the brigade and led with such energy that General Lee said of the brigade that "they deserved the thanks of the country—they saved his army." General Rodes declared of Grimes, "You have saved Ewell's Corps." When Ramseur fell at Cedar Creek, Grimes assumed command of the division, holding this position to the end.

Fighting through the Petersburg trenches, he participated with uncommon gallantry at Fort Stedman, riding a captured horse. When his line was broken on April 2, 1865, he rushed down the line on foot and, seizing a musket, joined in the fire upon the enemy until his troops, encouraged by his cool boldness, were able to recover the greater part of their line. At Saylor's Creek, he saved himself by riding up the precipitous banks amid a shower of bullets, and on the next day led his division in a splendid charge, recapturing guns from the enemy.

Fighting to the very last at Appomattox, he volunteered his division to cut through the enemy lines and clear the road to Lynchburg. At the last, his will to fight warred with his sense of honor, and he reluctantly agreed to the surrender. This last action is remembered in North Carolina's motto, "Last at Appomattox."

This beautiful silk flag was made in England according to the 1st (silk) pattern flags of the Army of Northern Virginia. It is 48" (hoist) x 53" (fly). The faded red field is crossed with 7¼"-wide blue bars edged with ⅝" white fimbriation. Twelve 5"-diameter stars are sewn to the cross. The flag is edged on three sides with 2½" gold silk and on the hoist with a 1" blue sleeve through which was passed a gold cord for fastening to the staff.

North Carolina Museum of History, Raleigh, N.C.

Fort Caswell

Fort Caswell lay thirty miles south of Wilmington on Oak Island at the mouth of the Cape Fear River. There was only one Federal caretaker on duty on January 9, 1861, when the Cape Fear Minutemen took the fort and demanded his surrender. With North Carolina still in the Union, this action proved to be an aggravation and embarrassment to Gov. John Ellis, who wired Col. John Cantwell, the commander of Wilmington's militia, to order the minutemen to move from the fort and restore Caswell to its Federal caretaker.

Order was restored, but on April 15, 1861, after sending his famous "You can get no troops" wire to Washington, Ellis sent new orders to Colonel Cantwell to seize Fort Caswell "without delay." For a second time, the hapless fort keeper was relieved of his duty.

According to family tradition, this flag was raised over Fort Caswell when it was captured by Colonel Cantwell's forces. It is 58" (hoist) x 62" (fly, remaining). The blue canton is 36" (hoist) x 33" (fly) and displays eight 7¼" white stars. The field is composed of red/white/red bars, which are 18"/18"/22", respectively.

The flag was found in the Cantwell home and donated to the Cape Fear Museum in 1999.

Cape Fear Museum, Wilmington, N.C.

Fort Caswell

South of Smithville, North Carolina, and occupying the easternmost part of Oak Island, Fort Caswell provided defense for the mouth of the Cape Fear River. Eventually armed with 32-pounders, 10-inch Columbiads, and one 150-pound Armstrong gun, Fort Caswell protected the approach between Oak Island and Smith's Island. Fort Caswell was evacuated January 16, 1865.

The nonstandard configuration for this 2nd National flag is actually standard for the British Naval Ensign, making it likely that this flag was made in England and brought through the blockade. It is 104" (hoist) x 171" (fly). In the British style, the canton occupies one-fourth of the field and is 52" x 85½". The blue bars forming the St. Andrews cross are 10" wide and are edged with 2¼" white fimbriation. The stars are sewn to the obverse, and the blue is cut away on the reverse to reveal the white of the star.

North Carolina Museum of History, Raleigh, N.C.

Fort Fisher

Fort Fisher was the largest, and probably the most important, fort in the Confederacy. Under the direction of Col. William Lamb, Fort Fisher went from a few sand batteries and a dozen guns in July 1862 to a most impressive earthen fort, stretching nearly a mile on its sea face with nearly fifty large-caliber guns. The defenses afforded by this fort and other batteries along the Cape Fear made Wilmington the most important port in the South and gave the Wilmington-Weldon Railroad the nickname "Lifeline of the Confederacy." Under the protection of Fisher's guns, blockade-runners came and went with great frequency, keeping hope alive for a struggling country.

With the fortunes of the Confederacy in decline on all fronts, the Union government made plans to capture Fort Fisher. The first assault came on December 24, 1864. After two days of fighting, Union commanders retired with a greater respect for the fort and the men within. The second attempt began on January 12, 1865. The fort was bombarded by Federal ships and assaulted on the land face by more than 3,300 Union infantry. On January 15, after six hours of fierce combat, the fort was surrendered to the Union forces.

This flag was captured by Union forces at the fall of the fort. (The reversed colors of the canton are most unusual.) It is 72" (hoist) x 137" (fly) with a 36" x 56" canton. The blue field of the canton is crossed with 5"-wide red bars edged with 2½" wide white fimbriation. Thirteen stars are sewn to the cross, with the center star being larger than the rest. The white field is made of four 18"-wide panels of white wool bunting.

Cape Fear Museum, Wilmington, N.C.

Salisbury Prison Garrison Flag

Salisbury Prison was the only Confederate prison in North Carolina. On November 2, 1861, the Confederate government purchased sixteen acres near Salisbury. The prison consisted of an old cotton factory building, six brick tenements, a large house, a smith shop, and a few other small buildings.

The first Union soldiers arrived shortly after the first battle at Manassas. Housing was spartan and the food was meager, but the yard was large and the early days of prison life were brightened with baseball games. Due to exchange and parole, overcrowding was not a problem until later in the war. As food supplies grew scarce, President Davis appealed to the Lincoln government for exchange of troops but was met with indifference.

As a war measure, Lincoln chose to keep the Southern prisoners. As the Federal government cancelled exchanges, life took a marked turn for the worse at Salisbury Prison. With overcrowding came disease and death. Thousands of graves mark the historic site at Salisbury today, a monument to Lincoln's disregard for his common soldier.

This 2nd National garrison-sized flag is 62" (hoist) x 113" (fly, remaining). The canton is 40" square and is crossed with 5½"-wide blue bars edged with 1" white fimbriation. Thirteen 4"-diameter stars adorn the cross. Along the hoist is a 1½" canvas sleeve.

North Carolina Museum of History, Raleigh, N.C.

Unidentified North Carolina Flag
New Berne

Little history accompanies this bunting-and-cotton North Carolina state flag. According to museum records, it was "purchased by S. W. Worthington from someone in Northern U.S." and is believed to have been "captured at the battle of New Berne in 1862." It is in relatively good condition except for a heavily deteriorated lower white panel.

The flag is 44" (hoist) x 75" (fly). The red field is 22" wide. These dimensions make the flag slightly longer than regulation, and this flag may be of private manufacture. The star is white cotton and the dates are painted in gold.

North Carolina Museum of History, Raleigh, N.C.

Unidentified North Carolina Flag
Wilmington

    Little history accompanies this North Carolina state flag except that it was donated to the Cape Fear Museum as part of the original United Daughters of the Confederacy collection. It was likely privately manufactured. It shares features of the first state flag in that it has a red hoist with a blue-over-white field. It shares one feature of the modern state flag in displaying *N* and *C* on either side of the center star.

    The flag is 22⅜" (hoist) x 34³⁄₁₆" (fly). The red bar is 11³⁄₁₆" wide. Centered side to side and slightly higher than center top to bottom is a 4⅜" diameter gold-painted star. On either side of the star are the letters *N* and *C*, painted white in 3¾"-high Roman uncial letters. Arched above and below the star are the two dates prescribed by the 1861 Flag Act, May 20, 1775, the signing of the Mecklenburg Declaration of Independence, and May 20, 1861, the date of North Carolina's departure from the Union. The dates are painted in white 2½"-high letters fluted slightly at the top and bottom.

Cape Fear Museum, Wilmington, N.C.

Unidentified 1st National

New Berne

This 1st National flag was auctioned to the public in the fall of 2001. According to tradition, the flag was captured by a Massachusetts regiment at the Battle of New Berne. No other history was attributed to the flag. Speculators have suggested that, since it was a plain, irregularly configured 1st National, it was likely not a military flag but was probably taken from a business or private home.

However, many North Carolina companies and regiments carried such flags. One similar flag, that of the 2nd North Carolina Battalion, was captured at the Battle of Roanoke. Without verification, one hypothesis is as good as another.

North Carolina units engaged at the Battle of New Berne were the 7th, 19th (Cavalry), 26th, 27th, 33rd, 35th, and 37th Regiments, with Brem's and Latham's batteries.

Private collection

Unidentified 1st National
Asheville

This hand-sewn 1st National flag was captured by the 2nd Michigan Infantry, at Asheville, around the same time that the flag of the Brevard Rangers was captured. It may or may not have ties to the 62nd Regiment North Carolina State Troops.

The flag is 32⅝" (hoist) x 62¾" (fly). The blue canton is 21¾" (hoist) x 23⅞" (fly) and displays twelve eight-pointed stars, each 4" in diameter. The stars are arranged in a circle of eleven, with one in the center. Three 10⅞"-wide bars, red/white/red, compose the field.

The flag was returned to North Carolina at a ceremony in Lansing, Michigan, on September 20, 1941.

North Carolina Museum of History, Raleigh, N.C.

Granbury Rifles

There were at least two flags constructed on this pattern, the only difference being the unit name. There was one flag made with "GRANBURY RIFLES" in the canton and another with the name "FRANKLIN RIFLES." The Franklin Rifles were organized in Louisburg and became Company L, 15th Regiment North Carolina State Troops. No company was enlisted in the name of Granbury Rifles. It could be that this flag played a role in determining the "inventor" of the Confederate 1st National.

In the *Confederate Veteran* (October 1915) is an article entitled "The Oldest Flag." In describing the flag of the Franklin Rifles, the author states that it was a "replica of the design submitted by Major [Orren R.] Smith to the Confederate Congress at Montgomery Ala., in February, 1861, was made in Petersburg, Va., under the direction of Mrs. Herbert Claiborne, who had been reared in Louisburg, and it was copied from Major Smith's design." The most obvious confusion would be that the flag is dated April 27, 1861. It seems unlikely that it could have been presented in February of that year.

The controversy over who actually designed the 1st National waged on into the 20th century, with the most contested designers being Major Smith from North Carolina and artist Nicola Marschall of Marion, Alabama. Evidence seems to lean toward Marschall but to some the argument has not been settled.

From a photograph in the North Carolina Museum of History, Raleigh, N.C.

1st National Variant
(unidentified)

This unidentified 1st National variant flag is associated with "J. E. Joyner," a name that is stamped along the edge, and with a lady named Margaret Stone. Its origin is likely Louisburg, North Carolina.

It is 23⅞" (hoist) x 30¼" (fly, not including a 1½"-wide canvas heading along the hoist). The blue canton is 15⅝" (hoist) x 12⅛" (fly). A single 3"-diameter star is sewn to the center of the canton and is surrounded by eleven 2⅜"-diameter stars in a rough oval that is 8¼" x 12½". The field is composed of red/white/red bars that are 7¹³/₁₆"/7¹³/₁₆"/8¼" respectively.

There is no known history associated with this flag.

North Carolina Museum of History, Raleigh, N.C.

3rd National Flag

Throughout the four-year history of the Confederate States of America, three national flags were approved by Congress. The third and last flag was created by an act of the Congress of the Confederate States and approved by President Davis on March 4, 1865. This was four years to the day of the creation of the first national flag and less than a month prior to the coming fall of Richmond. Only a handful of them were actually issued to the troops. Most of the 3rd National flags, like the one above, were privately made.

This beautiful silk 3rd National flag is 12½" (hoist) x 19¼" (fly). The canton is 7¼" (hoist) x 7⅜" (fly). The red field is crossed by 1½"-wide blue bars, which are edged with ½" white fimbriation. Evenly spaced on the cross are thirteen embroidered ¾"-diameter white stars. The red bar along the fly is 5¼" wide. Along the hoist is a 2" wide blue sleeve.

The flag was donated to the Cape Fear Museum in 1986 by Mr. Lawrence E. Johnson.

Cape Fear Museum, Wilmington, N.C.

Buncombe Riflemen
Co. E., 1st Regiment North Carolina Volunteers

On April 18, 1861, over a month before North Carolina would sever its ties with the Union, the Buncombe Riflemen were in formation in the streets of Asheville preparing to leave their

mountain home. It was an exciting occasion for the young men as well as the citizens of the town.

The *Asheville News* wrote, "The 'Buncombe Riflemen' are composed of first rate material and if they get into an engagement will reflect honor upon themselves and their native section. They will be led on by a brave and gallant officer. Captain McDowell is of pure metal, no mistake, and will contest every inch of ground with the enemy."

Pvt. Theodore Davidson said it was a "memorable day" and remembered Col. N. W. Woodfin's address as being "expressly stimulating," after which "Rev. Mr. Chapman closed the ceremonies with an eloquent prayer, commending them to care and protection of the Great Ruler of the Universe."

While a more appropriate flag was being created for the company, color bearer Alfred Baird carried the simple banner pictured above. Made of two strips of white cotton, it is 8¼" (hoist) x 31½" (fly). The letters are printed in black, likely a product of the presses of the *Asheville News*. The word "BUNCOMBE" is 13⅞" wide overall and composed of 1½"-high decorative floral-print block letters. There are three pairs of colored string ties; the top pair is red, the center white, and the bottom blue.

North Carolina Museum of History, Raleigh, N.C.

Buncombe Riflemen
Co. E, 1st Regiment North Carolina Volunteers

It was reported in the *Confederate Veteran* that this flag "was made and presented to [the company] by young ladies of Asheville—Misses Annie and Littie Woodfin, Fannie and Annie Patton, Mary Gains, and Kate Smith. The material was the silk dresses of three of the makers and donors; the colors, red, white, and blue. The presentation speech was made by Miss Annie Woodfin."

The silk flag was constructed in the pattern of the 1st National flag of the Confederacy, with overall dimensions of 37½" (hoist) x 49⅞" (fly). The canton is 24¾" (hoist) x 21⅝" (fly). Painted on the canton are eight 2¼"-diameter gold stars. The stars appear to be painted paper and adhered to the canton, a common mode of construction at this time.

The Buncombe Riflemen became Company E, 1st Regiment North Carolina Volunteers and were selected as the color company. This flag was carried on June 10, 1861, at Bethel, Virginia, in the first military action of the war. On June 17, 1861, the State Convention in assembly approved the following resolution:

"Resolved, That this convention, appreciating the valor and good conduct of the officers and men in the First Regiment of North Carolina Volunteers, does, as a testimonial of the same, authorize the said regiment to inscribe the word 'Bethel' upon their regimental colors."

No official regimental flag had been issued from the state at this time and Miss Annie Woodfin embroidered the honor on this flag of her creation.

North Carolina Museum of History, Raleigh, N.C.

Enfield Blues

Co. I, 1st Regiment North Carolina Volunteers

The company known as the "Enfield Blues" was organized at Enfield in Halifax County soon after the 1859 John Brown raid on Harpers Ferry. The company was ordered to Raleigh on April 23, 1861. Arriving on April 27, the company was stationed at the Camp of Instruction, where it was mustered into state service on May 13, 1861, as Company I of the 1st Regiment North Carolina Volunteers.

The flag of the Enfield Blues was made by Mrs. M. C. Whitfield and her daughters, Nannie and Emmie, and presented to the company shortly after its entry into state service. Obvious care was taken in the production of this silk flag; the fringe adds a finishing touch of elegance. But the emblems, stars, and letters were made of painted paper and have deteriorated badly. Perhaps the makers were rushed to have the flag ready at a certain date or perhaps it is an insinuation, as many believed, that hostilities would be over within "six months."

The flag is 40½" (hoist). Much of the canton's design on the above illustration is conjecture.

North Carolina Museum of History, Raleigh, N.C.

Chowan Dixie Boys/Dixie Rebels
Co. M, 1st Regiment North Carolina Volunteers

This company, known as the "Chowan Dixie Boys," and the "Dixie Rebels," was enrolled for active service at Edenton, Chowan County, on April 29, 1861. On May 26, the company was mustered into state service for twelve months of service. From Edenton, the company moved to Garysburg, where it arrived on June 15, 1861. Five days later it was assigned to the 1st Regiment North Carolina Volunteers as Company M. It was ordered to move from Garysburg to Richmond, Virginia, on June 22. From Richmond, the company proceeded to Yorktown, where it joined the regiment during the first week of August.

The silk flag of the Dixie Rebels is 37" (hoist) x 56" (fly) and is bordered on three sides with 2" gold fringe. The red field is 19" wide. The unit designation and unit name are painted on both sides in gold paint. Color bearer Pvt. Stephen W. Roberts donated the flag to the Museum of the Confederacy in 1896.

Museum of the Confederacy, Richmond, Va.

Albemarle Guards
Co. A, 1st Regiment, North Carolina State Troops

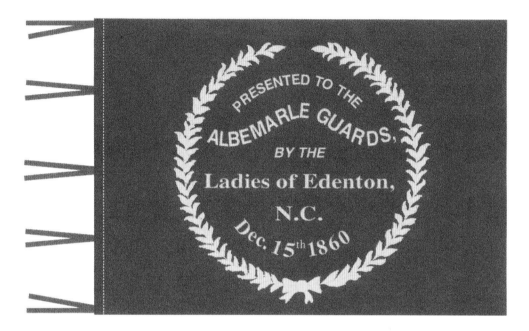

This company, known as the "Albemarle Guards," was raised in Chowan County and enlisted at Edenton on May 18, 1861. It tendered its service to the state and was ordered to Warrenton, where it became Company A of the 1st Regiment North Carolina State Troops on June 3, 1861.

This dark-blue silk flag was presented to the Albemarle Guards on December 15, 1860, during the early period of the company's formation. It is 40" (hoist) x 57" (fly).

Centered on the obverse is a 32"-diameter wreath, painted in gold, surrounding the presentation information, which is also painted in gold, "PRESENTED TO THE," in 1½"-high block letters; "ALBEMARLE GUARDS," in 2¾"- high block letters; "BY THE," in 2"-high block letters; "Ladies of Edenton," in 2¾"-high uppercase and 2"-high lowercase Roman letters; "N.C.," in 2"-high Roman letters; and "Dec. 15th 1860," in 2¼"-high uppercase and 1½"-high lowercase Roman letters and numerals.

There is some evidence of alteration to this flag, and it may have once had gold fringe on three edges. The silk is split and quite fragile.

Museum of the Confederacy, Richmond, Va.

Albemarle Guards
Co. A, 1st Regiment, North Carolina State Troops

This 1st National variant flag was carried by Company A, 1st Regiment North Carolina State Troops under the leadership of Capt. Tristrim L. Skinner. Promoted to major, Skinner was killed at Ellerson's Mill, Virginia, in June 1862.

This cotton flag is 40½" (hoist) x 114" (fly, remaining). The blue canton is 27" (hoist) x 28" (fly) and displays eleven 5½" white cotton stars in three columns of four/three/four, all oriented with one ray pointing to the staff. The field is composed of red/white/red bars. The red bars are both 13" wide and the white bar is 14" wide. There is a 10½"-high red cotton "C" sewn to the white bar. Next to the "C" is a torn space in which another letter was sewn, possibly an "I," the meaning of which could be "Confederate Infantry."

A ½" white cotton sleeve probably contained a rope for attachment to the staff.

Museum of the Confederacy, Richmond, Va.

1st Regiment
North Carolina State Troops

The 1st Regiment North Carolina State Troops was organized at Warrenton, on June 3, 1861. As a part of Ripley's/Ramseur's/Cox's Brigade, the regiment saw service in D. H. Hill's/Robert Rodes' Division, 2nd Corps, Army of Northern Virginia, participating in every campaign of that great army.

The 1st Regiment was surrendered at Appomattox, Virginia, on April 9, 1865.

This flag of the 1st Regiment is a Richmond Depot 3rd (bunting) issue and is 46" square. The red field is crossed by 5"-wide

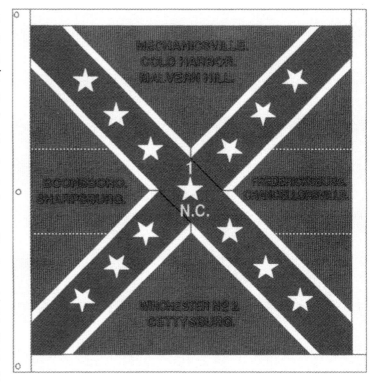

blue bars edged with ¾" white fimbriation. There are thirteen 3"-diameter stars spaced 6" apart. Painted in gold above and below the center star is the unit designation. The honors representing the regiment's service from Mechanicsville to Gettysburg are painted in blue block letters. The flag is bordered on three sides with 2"-wide white bunting. The hoist, now missing, was probably 2"-wide canvas pierced with three whipped eyelets.

This flag was captured at Spottsylvania Court House, May 12, 1864, by Pvt. George W. Harris, Company B, 148th Pennsylvania Volunteers.

North Carolina Museum of History, Raleigh, N.C.

Brown Mountain Boys
Co. A, 2nd Battalion North Carolina State Troops

This company, known as the "Brown Mountain Boys," was organized in Stokes County and enlisted May 4, 1861. It proceeded to Richmond, Virginia, where it joined Gen. Henry A. Wise's Legion and was assigned to Colonel Green's Independent Regiment. The regiment failed to complete its organization, and the companies were reorganized as the 2nd Battalion North Carolina State Troops on November 1, 1861. In January 1862, the battalion organization was completed and this company became Company A. Prior to January 1862, it had been referred to as Company A, Company B, and Capt. Milton Smith's Company.

The wool bunting flag of the Brown Mountain Boys is 68" (hoist) x 100" (fly). The blue canton is 44½" (hoist) x 38⅜" (fly). An eagle, cut from cotton, is sewn to the center of the canton and surrounded by twelve 4¾"-diameter stars. The unit inscription is embroidered on the bottom red bar. Four pairs of string ties were used to attach it to the staff.

This flag was captured by the 27th Massachusetts Volunteer Militia after the fall of Roanoke Island on February 8, 1862, and returned to North Carolina in 1988.

North Carolina Museum of History, Raleigh, N.C.

2nd Battalion

North Carolina State Troops

The 2nd Battalion North Carolina State Troops was organized at Richmond, Virginia, from the four companies raised for Green's Independent Regiment, Wise's Legion, and one independent company on November 1, 1861. The battalion's first assignment was to the Department of Henrico (North Carolina) and then to the District of the Cape Fear, Department of North Carolina.

They were part of the defense of Roanoke Island on February 8, 1862, when they were overwhelmed and captured by U.S. general Ambrose Burnside's invasion force. The above flag was captured by the 27th Regiment Massachusetts Volunteer Infantry and was kept in private hands until donated, in 1940, to the Connecticut Valley Historical Museum. It was presented to the State of North Carolina on November 19, 1988.

The flag of the 2nd Battalion is 33¾" (hoist) x 59¼" (fly). The field is composed of three bars, red/white/red, each 11¼" wide. The blue canton is 22½" (hoist) x 16½" (fly). Ten 3⅞"-4" white cotton stars are sewn to the canton, in a pattern that shows nine stars surrounding a central star.

The battalion was later paroled at Elizabeth City, reorganized, served throughout the war in the Army of Northern Virginia, and was surrendered at Appomattox on April 9, 1865.

North Carolina Museum of History, Raleigh, N.C.

2nd Regiment
North Carolina Volunteers

This regiment was organized for twelve months as the 2nd Regiment North Carolina Volunteers near Garysburg on May 15, 1861, and mustered into Confederate service there on May 18, 1861. The regiment was redesignated 12th Regiment North Carolina State Troops on November 14, 1861. After this date, some companies were reassigned and others picked up as the regiment prepared for active service.

This hand-sewn 1st National flag has "2nd N.C. Volunteers" stenciled on the cotton heading. It is 41" (hoist) x 57" (fly). The blue canton is 22" (hoist) x 27" (fly). The field of red and white bars are 13½"/13½"/14". There are eleven 4½" white stars sewn to the canton in an irregular oval. The flag was captured in battle, location unknown, and was returned after the war to Maj. S. V. Reid, who had served as commissary of subsistence for the Confederate States of America.

North Carolina Museum of History, Raleigh, N.C.

2nd Regiment
North Carolina State Troops

The 2nd Regiment North Carolina State Troops was organized at Camp Advance, Garysburg, in June 1861. They were mustered into state service there on June 19, 1861. They were assigned first to Walker's Brigade, Department of North Carolina, but are primarily associated with Anderson's/Ramseur's/Cox's Brigade, Hill's/Rode's Division, Army of Northern Virginia. From the Seven Days battles (June 1862), the 2nd Regiment served in every campaign of the Army of Northern Virginia, laying down its arms at Appomattox.

The beautiful silk State flag of the 2nd Regiment is a result of the efforts of Lawrence O'B. Branch in his role as quartermaster-general. It is 38" (hoist) x 53⅜" (fly) with a red cotton sleeve 2⅜" wide. The red field is 19⅜" wide and is ornately decorated with scrollwork showing the regimental designation on the obverse in gold letters shaded low and left in black.

Centered on the reverse of the red field is a six-pointed star, also shaded in black, above and below which are scrolls on which is written May 20, 1775, and May 20, 1861.

The flag was captured at Chancellorsville, Virginia, on May 3, 1863, by the 7th Regiment New Jersey Volunteers and was returned to the state in 1928.

North Carolina Museum of History, Raleigh, N.C.

2nd Regiment
North Carolina State Troops

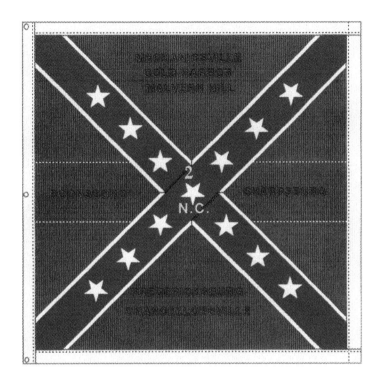

It could be that the 2nd Regiment North Carolina State Troops did not use a standard battle flag until the loss of their beautiful silk flag at Chancellorsville. Although other regiments of D. H. Hill's division received new Richmond Depot 3rd issue flags in April 1863, the 2nd Regiment did not receive this flag until after Chancellorsville. The honors on this flag, painted in blue block letters, reflect the service of the regiment from Mechanicsville through Chancellorsville.

This flag is 48" (hoist) x 49" (fly). The red field is crossed with 5"-wide blue bars edged with ⅝" white fimbriation. The flag is deteriorated and seven of the original thirteen 3½" stars remain nearly complete. The others are missing or severely fragmented. The flag is bordered on three sides with 1⅞"-wide bunting. Along the hoist is a 1¾"-wide canvas heading pierced with three whipped eyelets.

This flag was captured at the battle of Gettysburg.

National Park Service, Gettysburg, Pa.

Northampton Artillery
Co. A, 1st (Moore's) Light Artillery Battalion
Co. A, 3rd (Moore's) Light Artillery Battalion

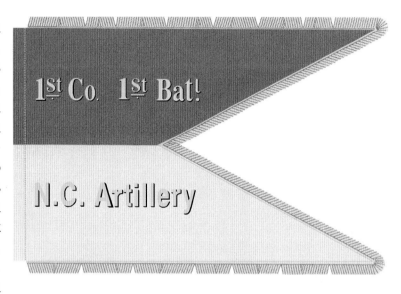

The Northampton Artillery, Capt. Andrew J. Ellis commanding, was organized as Company A, 1st Battalion North Carolina Light Artillery, in February 1862. The company was mustered into Confederate service as Company A, 3rd Battalion North Carolina Light Artillery at Camp Lee, Virginia, on May 20, 1862. This company served in Maj. John W. Moore's Battalion for the duration of the war.

In November 1863, the companies of the battalion were serving in separate locations, with Company A at Kenansville. Ellis' Battery was the only company to see action in 1864. While supporting General Martin's February attack on Newport Barracks, near Shepherdsville, Company A found itself in a unique situation. Captain Ellis ordered one of his guns to charge a lone Federal gun. Leading his men at a gallop, Ellis ordered his gunners to halt, wheel into battery, fire a few rounds, limber up, and then charge toward the enemy, only to go into battery again and fire. He kept this up until the enemy gunners fled and the gun was captured. It was a charge of artillery on artillery.

Company A was surrendered with the remains of the battalion by General Johnston at Durham Station on April 26, 1865.

This silk swallowtail flag of the Ellis Artillery is 44" (hoist) x 69½" (fly). It is red over gold and is edged all around with gold fringe. The unit designation is painted in gilt characters shaded lower and right. It was presented to the company in May 1861 and never surrendered.

North Carolina Museum of History, Raleigh, N.C.

Jeff Davis Rifles

Co. I, 3rd Regiment North Carolina State Troops

This company, known as the "Jeff Davis Rifles," was organized in Beaufort County and enlisted at Washington on May 10, 1861. It tendered its service to the state and was ordered to Garysburg, Northampton County, where it was assigned to the 3rd Regiment North Carolina State Troops as Company I.

This beautiful blue silk flag was made by Claudia A. Benbury, Sarah W. Williams, and Mrs. S. B. Waters, wife of Lt. Samuel B. Waters of the Jeff Davis Rifles. It is said to have been made of Mrs. Waters' wedding dress and a "calling dress." The flag is 47" (hoist) x 59" (fly) and is bordered on three sides with gold metallic fringe. Appliqued in the center are the initials "J. D. R." in fluted block letters surrounded by an oval of stars.

This flag was presented to the North Carolina Museum by Mary Louise Waters, granddaughter of Lieutenant Waters.

Museum of North Carolina History, Raleigh, N.C.

Roanoke Minutemen
Co. A, 4th Regiment North Carolina Volunteers

This company, known as the "Roanoke Minutemen," was from Warren and Halifax counties and enlisted at Littleton on March 30, 1861. On May 1, 1861, it left Littleton for Raleigh, where it arrived the same day. The next day, May 2, the company moved from Raleigh to Garysburg. There it was assigned to the 4th Regiment North Carolina Volunteers, later to become the 14th Regiment North Carolina State Troops.

The 1st National flag of the Roanoke Minutemen is 51" (hoist) x 65" (fly). The blue canton is 34" square. Painted in the center of the canton is an 11"-diameter wreath, above which is "ROANOKE" and below which is "MINUTE MEN." Surrounding the unit name is a 27"-diameter gold circle. Eleven 3⅜" stars arch above the circle. Below the circle in a reverse arch is "4th N.C. VOLS," to which was added a "1" after the reorganization, making the number "14."

North Carolina Museum of History, Raleigh, N.C.

Lexington Wild Cats
Co. I, 4th Regiment North Carolina Volunteers

This company, known as the "Lexington Wild Cats," was raised in Davidson County and enlisted at Lexington on May 14, 1861. On May 24, the company left Lexington for Garysburg, where it arrived the following day. There it was assigned to the 4th Regiment North Carolina Volunteers, later to become the 14th Regiment North Carolina State Troops.

The silk flag of the Lexington Wild Cats is a 1st National variant. It is 31" (hoist) x 47" (fly), which gives the flag a 4:6 ratio. Within a gold circle on the canton is a representation of the North Carolina state seal painted in oil paint in natural colors. Above the circle painted in gold block letters is "LEXING-TON." Below the circle is "WILD CATS." Three pairs of ties attached the flag to the staff.

North Carolina Museum of History, Raleigh, N.C.

4th Regiment
North Carolina Volunteers

This regiment was organized for twelve months as the 4th Regiment North Carolina Volunteers at Garysburg, Northampton County, on June 6, 1861. The regiment was redesignated as the 14th Regiment North Carolina State Troops on November 14, 1861.

This blue silk flag of the 4th Regiment Volunteers is 66" (hoist) x 70¼" (fly) and is edged on three sides with gold fringe. The obverse is constructed of three 22"-wide panels of blue silk on which is painted in gold "4TH REGIMENT OF/NORTH CAROLINA VOLUNTEERS" in 2½"-high block letters. Centered in the reverse is a 20"-diameter representation of the North Carolina seal, painted in natural colors.

This flag was presented to the regiment around the time of its formation, because the June 10 edition of the *Raleigh Standard* reported:

"Adjutant [Seaton E.] Gales of the 4th Regiment of N.C. Volunteers, having been on a visit to this family for a few days, left the City on Saturday morning last. He took down we learn, the standards of the Regiment. One, the Confederate flag [likely a 1st National]; the other, a blue silk banner, having on one side in the centre, the State seal, and on the other 'North Carolina—Fourth Regiment'."

The regiment was first assigned to the Department of Norfolk. In November 1861 the regiment, redesignated 14th North Carolina, was attached to Colston's Brigade, first in the Department of the Peninsula and then as a part of Longstreet's Division. They saw action at Yorktown, participated in the Seven Days Campaign around Richmond, and fought at South Mountain and Sharpsburg.

This flag was evidently still in use by the regimental color guard, perhaps as secondary colors, in September 1862. It was captured at Sharpsburg on September 17, 1862, by Cpl. George Nettleton, Company G, 5th New Hampshire Volunteers, during a desperate struggle between the two regiments in the infamous "Bloody Lane." Two hundred members of the 14th North Carolina were listed as dead, wounded, or missing at the end of the day.

Following the battle, the flag was sent to New Hampshire by the commander of the 5th Regiment, Col. Edward E. Cross. In 1914, Cross returned the captured banner to the State of North Carolina.

North Carolina Museum of History, Raleigh, N.C.

Pamlico Rifles
Co. I, 4th Regiment North Carolina State Troops

This company, known as the "Pamlico Rifles," was organized in Beaufort County and enlisted on June 25, 1861. It tendered its service to the state and was ordered to Camp Hill near Garysburg, Northampton County, where it was assigned to the 4th Regiment North Carolina State Troops, as Company I. The first commander of the company, Capt. William T. Marsh, was wounded at Sharpsburg and died September 24, 1862. The second commander, Capt. Edward Stanley Marsh, was wounded in the armpit and left lung at Chancellorsville.

This hand-sewn blue silk flag of the Pamlico Rifles is 47" (hoist) x 59" (fly) and is bordered on three sides with gold fringe. There are eleven stars appliqued to the field, two 4" diameter and nine 6" diameter, enclosed by a crescent made of gold metallic braid. The construction is very similar to the flag of the "Jeff Davis Rifles" and its manufacture is attributed to the same ladies.

North Carolina Museum of History, Raleigh, N.C.

4th Regiment
North Carolina State Troops

Organized at Camp Hill, near Garysburg, on May 16, 1861, and mustered into state service on June 28, 1861, the 4th Regiment North Carolina State Troops was sent to Virginia. In March 1862, the regiment was assigned to D. H. Hill's Division, Army of Northern Virginia, and saw action at Williamsburg, Seven Pines, Seven Days battles, South Mountain, Sharpsburg, Fredericksburg, and Chancellorsville, where the flag above was captured.

This Army of Northern Virginia Battle flag is a 2nd bunting issue, noted by its 5"-wide blue bars and orange flannel border. This issue of flags began in June 1862, with D. H. Hill's Division receiving the first disbursement. It is 48" (hoist) x 49" (fly). The red bunting field is crossed by 5" blue wool bunting bars edged with ½" white cotton fimbriation. There are thirteen 3½"-diameter white cotton stars, spaced 6" apart, creating a "compressed" look with the stars grouped in the center of the flag. The honor "WILLIAMSBURG" is printed in 3⅜"-high block letters, with serif, on a 4⅜" x 21⅝" cotton patch. The honor "SEVEN PINES!" is printed in similar-style 3¼"-high letters on a 4⅞" x 20¾" cotton patch.

The flag is edged on the top and bottom with 1½" orange flannel and on the fly with 1¾" orange flannel. Along the hoist is a 1½" cotton heading pierced with three whipped eyelets.

Museum of the Confederacy, Richmond, Va.

JOHN ALEXANDER STIKELEATHER

"When Sergeant Stikeleather was recommended for promotion to ensign on April 11, 1864, his recommendation noted the reason included his 'having borne the flag of [this] Regiment most gallantly in all the fights in which this command has participated since the battle of Seven Pines, having volunteered in that battle to become standard bearer after seven of the previous bearers had been killed or wounded.' Stikeleather was appointed ensign on April 21, 1864. He was wounded while carrying the colors at Cedar Creek, Virginia, on October 19, 1864."

4th Regiment
North Carolina State Troops

Gen. D. H. Hill's division received new Richmond Depot 3rd issue flags in April 1863. At this time, however, the 4th Regiment North Carolina State Troops was still using its 2nd bunting issue, the flag that was captured one month later at Chancellorsville. This flag was probably an individual flag issued to replace the one lost in battle.

Through the remainder of 1863, the 4th Regiment fought at Gettysburg, Bristoe, and the Mine Run Campaign. The following year the regiment saw action at Wilderness, Spottsylvania, North Anna, and Cold Harbor. Assigned to the Valley Campaign, the regiment fought at Monocacy, Snicker's Gap, and 3rd Winchester. In the Winchester fight, on September 19, 1864, the above flag was captured by Capt. John Seltzer of the 1st West Virginia Volunteer Cavalry.

This flag is 48½" (hoist) x 48¾" (fly). The red field is crossed by 4⅞" blue bars edged with ⅝" fimbriation. There are thirteen 3½" stars spaced 6" apart. The flag is bordered on three sides with 1⅞" white bunting and on the hoist with 1⅞" canvas pierced with three whipped eyelets.

North Carolina Museum of History, Raleigh, N.C.

4th Regiment
North Carolina State Troops

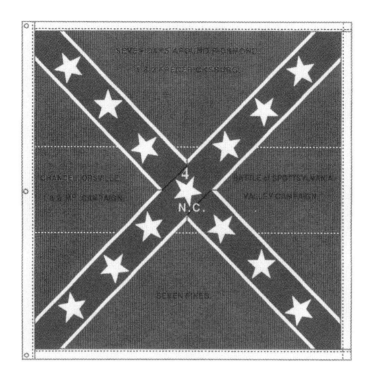

After Chancellorsville, the 4th Regiment North Carolina State Troops saw action in all the subsequent campaigns of the Army of Northern Virginia, from Gettysburg, at the Wilderness and Spottsylvania, through the Petersburg siege, and fought their last fights at Saylor's Creek and Farmville. The regiment was surrendered at Appomattox Court House on April 9, 1865.

Beginning in May 1864, the Richmond Depot began distribution of a 4th bunting issue of the Army of Northern Virginia battle flag. These flags were 51" square and crossed with 5"-wide blue bars, which were edged with ⅝" white cotton fimbriation. This flag of the 4th Regiment is of this 4th issue type. The honors, painted in blue block letters, reflect the regiment's service from the Seven Days battles through the battles of Monocacy and Winchester (Valley Campaign).

This flag was captured by Pvt. Asel Haggerty, Company A, 61st N.Y. Infantry, at Saylor's Creek, Virginia, on April 6, 1865.

North Carolina Museum of History, Raleigh, N.C.

Franklin Rifles
Co. L, 5th Regiment North Carolina Volunteers

This company, known as the "Franklin Rifles," was raised in Franklin County and enlisted at Louisburg on May 20, 1861. From Louisburg it was ordered to Franklinton and afterwards to Garysburg. The company was mustered into state service on June 12, 1861, and assigned to the 5th Regiment North Carolina Volunteers, later to become the 15th Regiment North Carolina State Troops, as Company L. The company served with this regiment until July 4, 1862, when it was transferred to the 32nd Regiment North Carolina State Troops and designated 2nd Company K.

This flag is illustrated in the October 1915 issue of *Confederate Veteran* in an article entitled "The Oldest Flag." The author contends that this flag was exhibited before the Flag Committee as evidence that Maj. Orren R. Smith of North Carolina be given credit for the original design of the 1st National flag. The author further states that the flag, "said to be a replica of the design submitted by Major Smith to the Confederate Congress at Montgomery, Ala., in February was made in Petersburg, Va., under the direction of Mrs. Herbert Claiborne, who had been reared in Louisburg, and that it was copied from Major Smith's design has been proved by sworn testimony."

North Carolina Museum of History, Raleigh, N.C.

5th Regiment
North Carolina State Troops

In a valiant and desperate charge at Williamsburg, Virginia, on May 5, 1862, the 5th Regiment North Carolina State Troops was decimated by Union fire and this silk flag was captured. This was the *first battle flag* captured in Virginia, and no procedure for processing had been developed by the War Department.

The flag was delivered upward through the chain of command until it made its way to the adjutant general of the U.S. Army. It was loaned out to be exhibited at the Chicago Sanitary Fair in October 1863. When it was returned, the flag was mixed with other captured flags arriving from Chattanooga and Knoxville and accidentally labeled as a "western flag."

When the flags were returned to the states in 1905, this flag was sent to Arkansas. It has been on display in the Old State House Museum in Little Rock as an "unidentified flag." In May 2002, historian Thomas L. McMahon made public his intensive research supporting his finding that this previously unidentified flag is indeed the missing flag of the 5th Regiment North Carolina State Troops.

On July 9, 2002, the flag was presented to the North Carolina State Museum as a gift from Arkansas.

This 1st silk issue flag is 47½" (hoist) x 46" (fly). The pink silk field is crossed by 7⅜"-wide blue bars, which are edged with ⅝"-wide white fimbriation. Twelve 4½"-diameter white stars are sewn to the cross at 7½" intervals. The flag is bordered on three sides with 2⅜"-wide gold silk and on the hoist with 1½"-wide blue cotton canvas, which is pierced with three whipped eyelets. The flag is fragile and the silk very fractured.

North Carolina Museum of History, Raleigh, N.C.

5th Regiment
North Carolina State Troops

The 5th Regiment North Carolina State Troops was organized at Camp Winslow, Halifax County, on June 20, 1861, and mustered into Confederate service there on July 15, 1861. After a brief period of time in Longstreet's Brigade, the regiment was assigned to Gen. Jubal Early's Brigade and was associated with this commander until its surrender at Appomattox.

The regiment participated in all of the major campaigns of the Army of Northern Virginia, a few of which included Seven Days, Manassas, and Sharpsburg. This flag was presented to the regiment in April 1863 and led the regiment through Gettysburg, Wilderness, and Chancellorsville. They participated in the 1864 Valley Campaign and returned to the Petersburg siege, fighting at Fort Stedman, where, in March 1865, this flag was captured by the 57th Massachusetts.

This Richmond Depot 3rd issue flag is 47" (hoist) x 36" (fly, remaining). The red field is crossed with 5"-wide blue bars edged with ½" white cotton fimbriation. Five 3½"-diameter stars remain of the original thirteen. Three sides were edged with 2"-wide white bunting. A 1¾" white canvas hoist is pierced with three whipped eyelets.

Museum of the Confederacy, Richmond, Va.

Rutherford Volunteers
Co. G, 6th Regiment North Carolina Volunteers

This company, known as the "Rutherford Volunteers," was from Rutherford County and enlisted at Rutherfordton on May 9, 1861. It was then mustered into service and assigned to the 6th Regiment North Carolina Volunteers, later to become the 16th Regiment North Carolina State Troops, as Company G. The company was commanded first by Capt. Champion Thomas Neal Davis and later by Capt. Lawson Pinkney Erwin.

The silk flag of the Rutherford Volunteers is a 1st National variant, the field of which is wrapped on three sides with a 1" gold ribbon, and is overall (discounting the fringe) 38" (hoist) x 80" (fly). The blue canton is 24" (hoist) x 26" (fly). Centered in the canton is a 14½"-diameter wreath surrounding a 4½"-diameter star. Painted in gold in an arch above the wreath is "IN GOD WE TRUST." In a reverse arch below the wreath is "VICTORY OR DEATH." The red/white/red bars composing the rest of the field are each 12" wide.

North Carolina Museum of History, Raleigh, N.C.

6th Regiment
North Carolina State Troops

The 6th Regiment North Carolina State Troops was organized on May 16, 1861, with Col. Charles F. Fisher as its first commander. In June, this beautiful, hand-sewn blue silk flag was carried by the regiment in the funeral of Gov. John W. Ellis and taken into battle the following month at Manassas. According to the regimental history, "it was not always used in battle, especially after battle flags had been distributed to the army. It was generally brought out on parades and general reviews; but it was not displayed at Appomattox. It was carefully preserved and brought to North Carolina."

The flag was 47⅝" (hoist) x 52½" (fly). The fly end is extremely deteriorated and the fly measurement is an approximation by doubling the distance from the hoist to the center star. The 3"-diameter star is embroidered, as is all of the lettering on the obverse. On the reverse is a cross-stitched representation of the North Carolina seal. Under the seal is an embroidered banner on which is embroidered "6th Infantry—State Troops."

The flag is edged on three sides with thick 4" gold fringe. A ⅞" dark-blue heading is pierced with six whipped eyelets for attachment to the staff.

North Carolina Museum of History, Raleigh, N.C.

Washington Grays

Co. A, 7th Regiment North Carolina State Troops
Co. K, 10th Regiment North Carolina State Troops

This company known as the "Washington Grays" was accepted in state service for twelve months on April 22, 1861, and assigned to the 7th Regiment North Carolina State Troops as Company A. An advance party from the company left for Portsmouth on the steamer *Petrel*. The main part of the company was celebrated with great fanfare at a ceremony in Washington. On Monday morning, May 20, 1861, an estimated crowd of 2,500 enthusiastic citizens were in attendance. A number of companies were present, including the Jeff Davis Rifles, the Southern Guards, the Home Guards, the Citizen's Guards, and a company of cadets.

The event was reported in great detail by the local paper:

"The Company was called at the beautiful grove of Mr. Jas. R. Grist. . . . The Grays were fully equipped and presented an appearance exceedingly creditable and it could not but be remarked that the expression on each countenance evinced a determination never to yield or show their backs to the enemy, if assailed. . . . The peculiar interest given to the occasion was the presentation of a beautiful flag by Miss Clara B. Hoyt on behalf of the ladies of Washington. Miss Hoyt delivered a very appropriate and elegantly concocted address to the Company, and displayed a warmth of manner, a graceful self possession, a clear and audible enunciation, and a partisan of feeling which none but a Southern Lady knows how to exhibit."

Accompanying the presenter were other young ladies, "dressed in white" and bearing insignia representing each of the other states in the Confederacy; they were Misses Mattie Hancock, Virginia (tobacco); Martha Fowle, North Carolina (pine); Bettie Hoyt, South Carolina (palmetto tree); M. A. Gallagher, Georgia (rice); Jennie McDonald, Alabama (cotton); Sarah Williams, Mississippi (cotton); Fannie Treadwell, Florida (magnolia); Julia Stevenson, Louisiana (sugarcane); Helen Shaw, Texas (lone star); Martha Hanks,

Tennessee; Mary L. Berry, Arkansas (nary one); Mary Fowle and Hattie Hoyt, flag bearers (badges of red, white, and blue); and Clara B. Hoyt, presenter (badge of Southern Confederacy).

Capt. Thomas Sparrow received the flag on behalf of the company. Sparrow, a native of Beaufort County, enlisted April 22, 1861. He was 42 years old. On May 16, he was appointed captain by Governor Ellis:

"Capt. Thos. Sparrow received the flag and responded in his usually happy manner, and with all in a style which showed at once the Gentleman, the Christian, and one who will prove himself the able and efficient commander. The programme was concluded with a prayer by the Rev. Edwin Geer."

That same morning, the Washington Grays departed on the steamer *Post Boy* for Ocracoke. On June 22, 1861, the company was transferred to the newly forming 10th Regiment North Carolina State Troops (1st Regiment North Carolina Artillery) and designated Company K. The company was mustered into Confederate service on August 20, 1861.

Nine days later, the company was captured at Hatteras Inlet and confined at Fort Warren, Boston Harbor, Massachusetts, until exchanged in January 1862. After their parole, the company was reformed at Wilmington and detailed on garrison duty at Fort French. It remained at Fort French through June 1863 and was transferred to Fort Lee, also near Wilmington. The company served at Fort Lee until May 1864.

A detachment of the company under Lt. John M. Blount was sent to Weldon. The rest of the company was transferred to Smithville. For a few months, the company was split up into detachments serving where they were needed in the Wilmington/Fort Fisher area. In December 1864, the company was sent to Fort Fisher.

Most of the company was captured at Fort Fisher on January 15, 1865. The remainder, serving as infantry, was surrendered by Joseph E. Johnston at Durham Station on April 26, 1865.

The beautiful hand-sewn silk flag, presented to the company on May 20, 1861, is 54" (hoist) x 92" (fly). The blue canton is 35½" (hoist) x 37½" (fly). A circle of ten 7"-diameter stars surrounds one 8"-diameter star on the canton. The field is composed of red/white/red bars each 18" wide. The flag is bordered on three sides with gold fringe. Along the hoist are fourteen whipped eyelets.

North Carolina Museum of History, Raleigh, N.C.

7th Regiment
North Carolina State Troops

The 7th Regiment North Carolina State Troops was organized at Camp Mason, near Graham, on August 17, 1861. As a member unit of Lawrence O'B. Branch's Brigade, the regiment saw service in the Department of North Carolina, participating in the Battle of New Berne. In May 1862, the regiment traveled with the brigade to Virginia, where they saw action at Hanover Court House on May 27, 1862. As a part of A. P. Hill's division, they participated in the Seven Days Campaign around Richmond and later that summer fought at Cedar Mountain, 2nd Manassas, and Sharpsburg.

In December 1862, Branch's Brigade was issued battle flags from the Richmond Depot. These 3rd (bunting) issue flags were strikingly marked with white scalloped block letters, with one group paralleling the four edges and one group encircling the center of the cross. Of these beautiful flags, all of Branch's issue have survived, even though the one above is only a fragment. The remnant is 3" high and bears the honor "HANOVER" on the obverse and "SHARPSBURG" on the reverse. The specific honors on the flag of the 7th regiment cannot be known from this fragment but more complete versions of this flag can be seen in the articles on the 18th, 28th, and 37th Regiments. The December 1862 issue flag of the 7th Regiment would have been similar.

North Carolina Museum of History, Raleigh, N.C.

7th Regiment
North Carolina State Troops

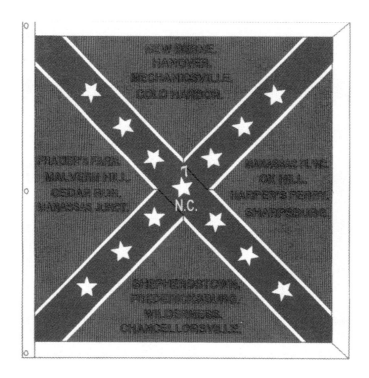

The 7th Regiment North Carolina State Troops received this flag as part of the June 1863 distribution of 3rd (bunting) issue flags to A. P. Hill's Light Division. This flag reflects the regiment's service from New Berne to Chancellorsville.

It is 47" (hoist) x 47" (fly). The red bunting field is crossed with 5"-wide blue bars edged with ½" white cotton fimbriation. Thirteen 3½"-diameter white cotton stars are sewn at 6" intervals to the St. Andrew's cross. The honors are painted to the red field in blue block letters.

This flag was captured at Gettysburg on July 3, 1863, by Pvt. John E. Mayberry, Company F, 1st Delaware Volunteers. This flag, War Department capture number 44, was returned to North Carolina along with the general return of flags on March 25, 1905.

North Carolina Museum of History, Raleigh, N.C.

8th Regiment
North Carolina State Troops

The 8th Regiment North Carolina State Troops was organized on September 14, 1861, at Camp Macon near Warrenton, North Carolina. Six days later, it was mustered into Confederate service with eight companies (Companies E and F were assigned on September 28). They were first attached to the Department of North Carolina. On February 7-8, 1862, the regiment participated in the one-sided defense of Roanoke Island. Completely overwhelmed by the massive assault, the regiment was captured. The above flag was captured and claimed by the 24th Massachusetts Infantry Regiment.

This flag was presented to the 8th Regiment as part of the initial disbursement of ten flags arranged by L. O'B. Branch. It is 39" (hoist) x 62" (fly) and is constructed of silk, ornately decorated with painted scrolls and flourishes. This flag is similar to most of the 1st issue flags, with the regimental designation on the obverse. On the reverse red field is a six-pointed star, above and below which are the dates prescribed by the Flag Act.

North Carolina Museum of History, Raleigh, N.C.

JACOB R. BARNHARDT

Jacob Barnhardt, a farmer from Cabarrus County, enlisted August 6, 1861, for the war. He was 23. He was captured with the regiment's colors at Roanoke Island. Paroled and exchanged, he returned to the regiment and was promoted to corporal on December 10, 1863, and to sergeant on April 20, 1864.

In the summer of 1864, the Confederate government authorized the rank of ensign for color bearers. Barnhardt was promoted to ensign on June 17, 1864.

At the battle of Fort Harrison, Virginia, on September 30, 1864, while bearing the colors, Ensign Barnhardt was wounded in the left leg. He was hospitalized at Fort Monroe until confined at Point Lookout prison.

He was released from prison on June 8, 1865.

8th Regiment
North Carolina State Troops

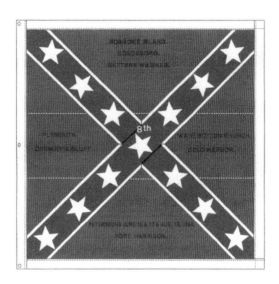

The 8th Regiment North Carolina State Troops after its exchange was reorganized at Camp Mangum in September 1862. Assigned to Clingman's Brigade, Department of North Carolina, the regiment saw service at Goldsboro Bridge and, in the summer of 1863, served in the defense of Battery Wagner at Charleston, South Carolina. In April 1864, the regiment participated in the recapture of Plymouth, North Carolina. In this battle, the color bearer, F. J. Perkins, was killed. In May 1864, Clingman's Brigade was attached to Hoke's Division, Army of Northern Virginia, and saw action at Drewry's Bluff, Cold Harbor, Petersburg, Globe Tavern, and Fort Harrison.

At Fort Harrison, the wounded color bearer, J. R. Barnhardt, found that he could not escape capture and tore to pieces the old flag that had seen so much service rather than allow its capture. Returning to the Carolinas, the regiment took part in the defense of Fort Fisher in January 1865 and was surrendered at Durham on April 26, 1865.

At the surrender, color bearer J. V. Fisher saved the above flag from capture and brought it home. It is of the Richmond Depot 4th (bunting) issue and is 46½" (hoist) x 51" (fly). It was issued in the fall of 1864 and is one of two 4th issue flags that were issued with honors.

Private collection

Cabarrus Rangers

Co. F, 9th Regiment North Carolina State Troops/ Co. F, 1st North Carolina Cavalry Regiment

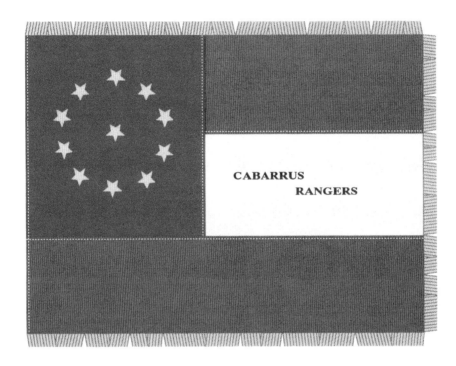

This company, known as the "Cabarrus Rangers," was organized for the war at Concord, Cabarrus County, beginning June 15, 1861. It was initially composed of men from Cabarrus County under the leadership of Capt. Rufus Barringer. On July 3, 1861, the company set out for Asheville, where the western companies of the regiment had been ordered into camp for drill and discipline. About August 1, 1861, the companies at Asheville were moved to Camp Beauregard, at Ridgeway, Warren County. This camp had been designated a regular school of cavalry instruction, and it was here that the 9th Regiment North Carolina State Troops (1st Regiment North Carolina Cavalry) was formed on August 12, 1861.

The 1st National flag of the Cabarrus Rangers is 32½" (hoist) x 44¾" (fly). The canton is 21¾" (hoist) x 20" (fly) and displays eleven 2"-diameter gold stars, one in the center of a 12"-diameter circle of ten. The unit name is painted on the center white bar.

Cabarrus County Historical Society, Concord, N.C.

9th Regiment North Carolina State Troops

1st Regiment North Carolina Cavalry

The 1st Regiment North Carolina Cavalry was organized at Camp Beauregard, Ridgeway, Warren County, on August 12, 1861, and mustered into Confederate service at Richmond, on October 21, 1861. Originally assigned to the Cavalry Brigade, Potomac District, the regiment went on to serve under various brigade commanders, including their own Robert Ransom, Wade Hampton, James B. Gordon, and Rufus Barringer.

Their term of service took the regiment into an amazing number of encounters with the enemy, including the Seven Days Campaign, Brandy Station, Hanover, Manassas Junction, Wilderness, Petersburg, Reams' Station, and Dinwiddie Court House. The regiment was surrendered with the Army of Northern Virginia at Appomattox on April 9, 1865.

The flag of the 1st North Carolina Cavalry is an Army of Northern Virginia variant. It is believed that when General Gordon was mortally wounded at Yellow Tavern, this flag was sent home as a covering for his coffin. It is 34" square. The red field is crossed with 4"-wide blue bars on which are sewn thirteen 2¼"-diameter eight-pointed stars. The cross is bordered with 1" white fimbriation. The "N" is 2¼" high x 2"-wide. The "1" is 2¼" high x 1¼" wide. The "C" is 2¼" high x 1½" wide. The flag is bordered with 2"-wide orange flannel. It was never captured.

Private collection

Manly's Battery

Co. A, 10th Regiment North Carolina State Troops/ Co. A, 1st Regiment North Carolina Artillery

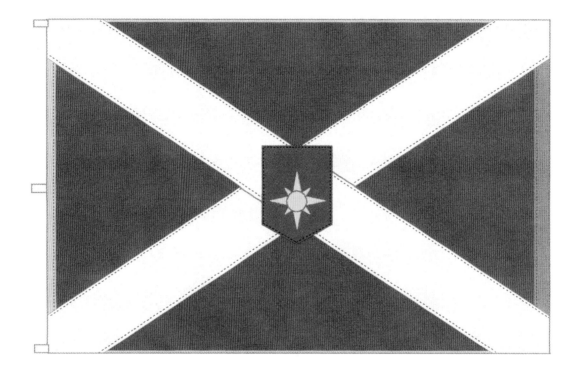

This unusual flag is probably the only surviving example of one of the Confederate Congress' many attempts to come up with a national flag. A Joint Committee on Flag and Seal was appointed by both houses of the first Confederate Congress, and on April 19, 1862, it submitted its recommendation as a joint resolution:

"Resolved by the Congress of the Confederate States of America, That the flag of the Confederate States shall be as follows: A red field, charged with a white saltier, having in the centre the device of the sun, in its glory, on an azure ground, the rays of the sun corresponding with the number of States composing the Confederacy."

After much debate, the House of Representatives voted 39 to 21 to postpone further consideration of the resolution, which the Senate never formally discussed. The bill died in Congress.

One year earlier, in April 1861, a battery of artillery was organized in Raleigh and was named the Ellis Light Artillery in honor of the governor of the state, John W. Ellis. The commander was Capt. Stephen D. Ramseur. The battery was mustered into Confederate service on May 8, 1861, and was designated Company A, 10th Regiment North Carolina State Troops. On May 20, 1861, the men fired the salute that signaled North Carolina's departure from the Union.

On August 2, 1861, the company left North Carolina for Virginia. After a period of drill and guard duty around Smithfield, Virginia, the battery saw its first action as a part of the Peninsula campaign. On April 4, 1862, while the Confederate Congress was in debate over a new flag, Ramseur's Battery engaged a Union battery at Dam No. 1. This six-gun Federal battery was silenced by Company A and captured by Confederate infantry.

Shortly before this action, Captain Ramseur was promoted and given command of the 49th North Carolina Regiment. Lt. Basil C. Manly was promoted and elected to command the battery. The men held a meeting at Camp Fisher and decided from that point on the battery would be called "Manly's Battery." It was probably around this time that the new flag, made by ladies of Wake County, North Carolina, according to the design being debated at that time in Richmond, was presented to the battery.

The flag is 28½" (hoist) x 44⅜" (fly). It was beautifully made, the field being of red brocade cloth and crossed with 5½"-wide silk bars forming a St. Andrew's cross. The blue shield (or "ground") is 6¼" wide x 8¼" high. The golden sun in the center is 1⅝" diameter, the long rays being 5" point to point, and the shorter rays being 3½" point to point. Along the fly is a 1¼" rose-colored protective cotton edging. The flag is edged along the top and bottom with ¼" gold ribbon, and along the hoist with a ¾"-wide gold heading.

Though never officially approved, this flag survives as one of a kind, and one of the more strikingly attractive patterns considered by the Confederate Congress.

Manly's Battery remained with the Army of Northern Virginia, seeing action in the Seven Days battles, at South Mountain, Sharpsburg, Fredericksburg, Chancellorsville, Gettysburg, the Wilderness, Spottsylvania Court House, North Anna, Cold Harbor, and the siege of Petersburg. The battery was surrendered at Appomattox on April 9, 1865.

North Carolina Museum of History, Raleigh, N.C.

Topsail Rifles
Co. H, 10th Regiment North Carolina State Troops/ Co. H, 1st Regiment North Carolina Artillery

This company, known as the "Topsail Rifles," was organized in Carteret County soon after Lincoln's election. After tendering its service to the state on May 21, 1861, the company was designated Company H, 10th Regiment North Carolina State Troops and stationed at Fort Macon. Alternately known as "Pool's Battery," "Manson's Battery," and "Miller's Battery," it also served the State as Company C, 2nd Regiment North Carolina State Troops.

Captured at the surrender of Fort Macon on April 28, 1862, the company was paroled in June and exchanged in August. It served as infantry from August to December, taking part in battles at Washington (North Carolina), Kinston, and Goldsboro Bridge. From December the company served as engineers engaged in the construction and deployment of pontoons.

A detachment served in the battle of Plymouth in April 1864. Afterward the company served in the defense of Plymouth until its fall in October and from there retired to Fort Branch, remaining there until April 10, 1865. The company was surrendered at Stantonsburg, Wilson County, North Carolina, on April 25, 1865.

The silk flag of Company H was captured at Fort Macon, April 26, 1862, by Company E, 5th Rhode Island Volunteers and presented by survivors of that company to the survivors of Company H at Raleigh in March 1906.

North Carolina Museum of History, Raleigh, N.C.

Washington Grays
Co. K, 10th Regiment North Carolina State Troops
Co. K, 1st Regiment North Carolina Artillery

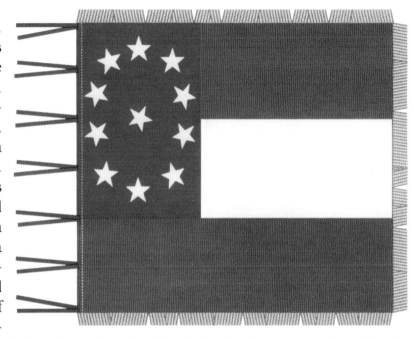

Enlisted as infantry, the Washington Grays were transferred to the artillery on June 22, 1861, and were redesignated Company K, 10th Regiment North Carolina State Troops. Their first post was Fort Hatteras, located on the southwestern tip of Hatteras Bank, a square redoubt, constructed of sand and reinforced with turf from adjoining marshes. Hatteras was the first stepping stone in the Union's plan to capture North Carolina's sounds. Properly outfitted, it could have defended itself. Its armament of twelve 32-pounder smooth bores, would prove inadequate and unfortunate.

On August 29, 1861, a Union fleet lay offshore, out of range of the fort's guns, and with superior cannons, pounded Fort Hatteras to pieces. Finally, Confederate Flag Officer Barron raised the white flag. Confederate losses were a 1,000 stand of arms, 35 cannons, 2 forts, and 680 men, among them the men of the Washington Grays. (See Co A, 7th Regiment N.C.S.T.)

At the battery's capture, Capt. Thomas Sparrow returned this flag to his wife. It is 59⅝" (hoist) x 68" (fly). The blue canton is 39⅛" (hoist) x 25½" (fly). Eleven 5"-diameter stars are arranged in an oval on the canton, one in the center surrounded by ten. The flag is bordered on three sides with gold fringe. Along the hoist are seven sets of blue ties.

North Carolina Museum of History, Raleigh, N.C.

Yadkin Gray Eagles

Co. B, 11th Regiment North Carolina Volunteers
Co. A, 1st Battalion Sharpshooters

The Yadkin Gray Eagles were the first company raised in Yadkin County, N.C. Upon their arrival in Virginia, the company was mustered into Confederate service as Company B, 11th Regiment North Carolina Volunteers, later the 21st Regiment North Carolina State Troops.

At the reorganization of the army at Manassas in February 1862, Companies B and E were detached from the regiment and redesignated Companies A and B, 1st Battalion North Carolina Sharpshooters. Lt. Reuben E. Wilson of Company B was promoted to captain of the company. When the battalion commander was promoted to regimental command, Wilson was promoted to major and given command of the battalion.

This battalion was an active participant in nearly every battle fought by the Army of Northern Virginia, from Manassas to Appomattox, and because of what was called their "peculiar and efficient drill," engaged in many skirmishes in which the main army did not participate.

The above flag was presented to the Yadkin Gray Eagles upon their departure for Virginia. It was made from the silk dresses of the young ladies of the county and presented to the company by Miss Lou Glenn, later Mrs. Joseph Williams. The captain, in receiving it on behalf of the company, closed his speech with these words:

"When this cruel war is over, Miss Lou,
This flag untarnished shall be returned to you."

It is 40½" (hoist) x 53⅜" (fly). The reverse is an irregularly configured 1st National pattern. The canton is 19½" (hoist) x 23¾" (fly). On the canton are thirteen 4"-diameter embroidered stars arranged with one center star encircled by eleven. The top red bar is 13¼", the bottom red bar is 12⅝", and the white background composing the center bar is 14⅝". On the bottom red bar is embroidered, "YADKIN GRAY EAGLES."

The obverse is solid white except for the embroidered motto, "WE SCORN THE SORDID LUST OF PELF/AND SERVE OUR COUNTRY FOR OURSELF." Instead of fringe, the three edges are adorned with ruffles.

This is perhaps the only company flag that was carried through twenty-six battles, from Manassas to Appomattox, through the war and returned, "untarnished," to its donors. In 1898, the daughter of Mrs. Williams, Mrs. Robert Daniels, was the guardian of the flag. The flag was later presented to the state.

North Carolina Museum of History, Raleigh, N.C.

MAJOR REUBEN EVERETT WILSON

On August 9, 1862, in a charge against the enemy near Warrenton, Va., Major Wilson was severely wounded when a minie ball broke both bones of the right forearm. At the same time, his left leg was shattered below the knee by a grape-shot, which disabled him for several months. On April 2, 1865, in a charge at Petersburg, he was again wounded, his left leg being cut off by a shell. He was hospitalized, paroled on April 21, rearrested, and taken to Libby Prison, where he remained until December 20, 1865.

When life returned to normal, Major Wilson ran a successful mercantile business in Augusta, Ga.

The photograph is a post-war picture of Major Wilson flanked by the flag of his company, the Yadkin Gray Eagles.

Forsythe Rifles
Co. D, 11th Regiment North Carolina Volunteers

This company, known as the "Forsythe Rifles," was from Forsythe County and enlisted at Winston and Salem on May 22, 1861. It tendered its service to the state and was ordered to Danville, Virginia, where it was assigned to the 11th Regiment North Carolina Volunteers, later to become the 21st Regiment North Carolina State Troops, as Company D. The company was commanded by Capt. Alfred Horatio Belo, who was defeated for reelection around April 26, 1862, and later served as lieutenant. colonel of the 55th Regiment North Carolina State Troops.

This silk flag is 43½" (hoist) x 68" (fly) with gold fringe along the fly edge only. The canton is 29¼" (hoist) x 29½" (fly) and displays fifteen six-pointed 4"-diameter gold stars. The field is composed of red/white/red bars, which are 14½"/14¾"/14½", respectively. A red and white cravat with each end displaying four embroidered stars decorates the 3⅞"-wide hoist sleeve. Embroidered in gold script on the lower fly edge is "Forsythe Rifles, N.C." The reverse of the flag is a white field on which is embroidered "Victory or Death."

This beautiful flag was made by Bettie and Laura Lemley; Mollie and Carrie Fries; and Nellie Belo, sister of the company commander. According to

Captain Belo, this flag was presented to the unit by six young ladies of Salem *"on the steps of my father's homestead.."* The 11th North Carolina adopted the flag as its regimental colors and carried it during the Battle of First Manassas. One soldier wrote home that *"Our flag has been generally admired by all who have examined it, indeed it is considered 'The Flag' among all others."*

This flag was removed from general use about the same time that the 11th Regiment Volunteers was redesignated the 21st Regiment North Carolina State Troops. A rare photograph of a Confederate company in formation shows the Forsythe Rifles on line near Danville, Virginia, around June or July 1861, shortly before departing for Manassas. Although indistinct, the photograph shows the canton and lower bar of the flag as well as the white reverse as it folds over the front of the flag.

Museum of the Confederacy, Richmond, Va.

11th Regiment
North Carolina State Troops

The 11th Regiment North Carolina State Troops was organized at Camp Mangum on March 31, 1862. The regiment served in the Department of North Carolina and was attached to Pettigrew's Brigade in December 1862. In this brigade, a part of D. H. Hill's command, the regiment participated in the New Berne and Washington campaign in the spring of 1863. Pettigrew's Brigade traveled to Virginia in May 1863, and from Gettysburg to Appomattox the service of the 11th Regiment paralleled that of the Army of Northern Virginia.

The flag of the 11th Regiment is a Richmond Depot 2nd bunting issue. These flags were generally 48" square, although this example measures 47" on the hoist. The fly edge is tattered but the flag likely was 47" square. The red field is crossed with 5" blue bars on which were thirteen 3½"-diameter stars, of which nine remain. The cross is edged with ½" white cotton fimbriation. The flag is bordered on three sides with 2" orange bunting border. A 2"-wide canvas heading, pierced with three whipped eyelets, serves as flag attachment.

This flag has no record of capture and was likely presented to the State Museum around 1920.

North Carolina Museum of History, Raleigh, N.C.

Cleveland Guards

Co. E, 12th Regiment North Carolina State Troops

This company known as the "Cleveland Guards" was raised in Cleveland County and enlisted at Shelby on April 22, 1861. It tendered its service to the state and was ordered to Garysburg, where it was assigned to the 12th Regiment North Carolina State Troops. The company was mustered in as Capt. Augustus W. Burton's Company and was designated Company D, Company H, and Company I, before it was designated Company E. This company functioned as part of the regiment for the duration of the war.

This 30" (hoist) x 64" (fly) silk 1st National variant flag was made by the ladies of Shelby and presented to the company in May 1861. The unit designation is embroidered on the white bar in red Old English letters. The flag was captured by the 9th Massachusetts Volunteers at the battle of Hanover Courthouse on May 27, 1862. Sent to Boston, the flag was returned to Shelby in 1898 and presented to the United Daughters of the Confederacy by the survivors of the company.

North Carolina Museum of History, Raleigh, N.C.

12th Regiment
North Carolina State Troops

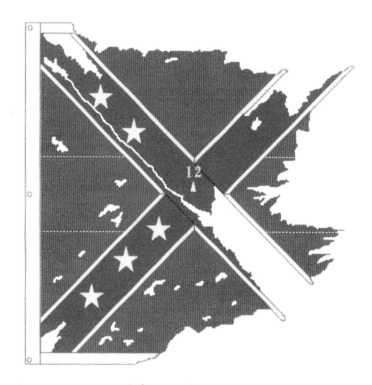

This regiment was organized for twelve months as the 2nd Regiment North Carolina Volunteers near Garysburg on May 15, 1861. There they were mustered into Confederate service three days later. The regiment was redesignated as the 12th Regiment North Carolina State Troops on November 14, 1861. First assigned to the Department of Norfolk and then to the Army of Northern Virginia, the regiment participated in every campaign of that army, surrendering at Appomattox Court House on April 9, 1865.

This hand-sewn battle flag is a type of 3rd issue from the Richmond Depot. This flag was captured by Sgt. E. D. Woodbury, Company E, 1st Vermont Cavalry and was assigned War Department capture number 163. The number places the capture around October 19, 1864. At this time the regiment was in action at Cedar Creek.

North Carolina Museum of History, Raleigh, N.C.

JOHN W. ARRINGTON

John Arrington enlisted in Company E, 12th Regiment (Cleveland Guards), on February 23, 1862. He was eighteen. As color bearer for the regiment he was nominated for the Badge of Distinction for gallantry at the Battle of Chancellorsville, May 1-3, 1863. He was wounded at Spottsylvania on May 10, 1864, and died of his wounds ten days later.

Flanner's Battery
Co. F., 13th Battalion North Carolina Artillery

The Richmond Depot distributed a 7th issue of battle flags in January and February of 1865. Because of the late manufacturing date, this 7th-issue flag displays a broad spectrum of battle honors from New Berne (March 14, 1862) to Darbytown Road (October 13, 1864). The battle honors represent the service of this battery under all three of its organizations.

The North Carolina Branch Artillery was organized in Craven County and mustered in at New Berne on January 30, 1862. The battery was reorganized as Company H, 40th Regiment North Carolina State Troops/3rd North Carolina Artillery Regiment on September 9, 1863. The battery was again reorganized as Company F, 13th Battalion North Carolina Artillery (Flanner's Battery) on November 4, 1863. Flanner's Battery was surrendered at Appomattox on April 9, 1865.

This flag is 48" (hoist) x 48" (fly). The red field is crossed with 4⅜"-wide blue bars, which are edged with ½"-wide white fimbriation. Eighteen battle honors, applied in blue paint, are displayed on the red field. There are thirteen 4¼"-diameter stars sewn to the cross and spaced at 6½" to 7½" centers. The flag is bordered on three sides with 2¼"-wide white bunting and on the hoist with 2"-wide canvas pierced with three whipped eyelets.

Cape Fear Museum, Wilmington, N.C.

13th Regiment
North Carolina State Troops

This regiment was organized as the 3rd Regiment North Carolina Volunteers at Garysburg on May 27, 1861. They were mustered into Confederate service for twelve months at Suffolk, Virginia, on June 1, 1861, and reorganized as the 13th Regiment North Carolina State Troops.

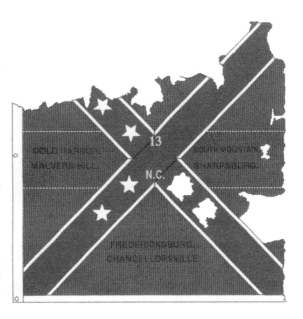

The regiment's first commander was the gallant William Dorsey Pender. As a part of Colston's Brigade, Longstreet's Corps, the regiment probably received a 1st bunting issue flag similar to the surviving flag of the 14th Regiment. As a part of Garland's/Pender's/Scales' brigade, the 13th Regiment saw action in every campaign associated with the Army of Northern Virginia. The regiment was surrendered at Appomattox, at which time this flag, with a capture number of 428, was probably surrendered.

The flag is an Army of Northern Virginia 3rd bunting issue from the Richmond Depot.

North Carolina Museum of History, Raleigh, N.C.

WILLIAM F. FAUCETTE

Alamance County native William Faucette enlisted in Co. E, 3rd N.C.V. (later 13th N.C.S.T.) in May 1861. He was promoted from private to color sergeant in June 1863. At Gettysburg, on July 1, 1863, Faucette carried the regimental flag during the attack against Union troops. He was struck in the left arm by an artillery shell and captured by Federal soldiers. His severe wound necessitated amputation of his arm, and he spent eight months in prison. Faucette was exchanged in March 1864 and paroled at Greensboro in May 1865.

13th Regiment
North Carolina State Troops

Three features of this well-made 2nd National pattern flag of the 13th Regiment North Carolina State Troops indicate the likelihood of English manufacture. The honors are painted in a more ornate pattern than is common to most regimental flags; the flag is machine-sewn and the 36"-wide panel in the field is uncommonly wide for Southern looms of that period. This flag could have been commissioned as a presentation flag and used for drill and ceremonial reviews.

For some reason, possibly the severe battle deterioration of the regular flag, this flag was used in battle at the Wilderness, May 6, 1864, where it was captured by Sgt. Stephen Wrought, Company A, 141st Pennsylvania Volunteers.

It is 46⅜" (hoist) x 65⅜" (fly, not including canvas heading). The canton is 28" square. The red bunting is crossed with 4" wide blue bars which are edged and wrapped on the ends with ½" white fimbriation. Thirteen 3½" white stars are sewn to the cross. The honors are painted in gold, and shaded black low and left. The inclusion of "GETTYSBURG" would indicate a production date later than July 1863. The white field is composed of two panels of bunting, one wide panel and one 10⅝" lower panel. Along the hoist is a 2⅝"-wide canvas heading pierced with three whipped eyelets.

After its capture, this flag was returned to the War Department and given capture number 123.

North Carolina Museum of History, Raleigh, N.C.

14th Regiment
North Carolina State Troops

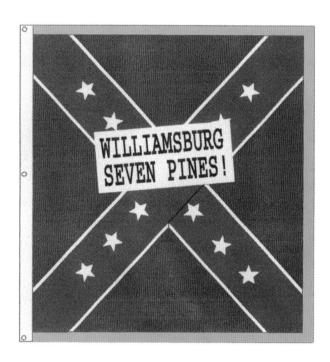

Organized for twelve months as the 4th Regiment North Carolina Volunteers at Garysburg on June 6, 1861, the regiment was redesignated 14th Regiment North Carolina State Troops on November 14, 1861. The regiment was reorganized for the war on April 27, 1862.

In June 1861, the regiment was assigned to the Department of Norfolk. From this time, the 14th Infantry served in Virginia, first in Colston's Brigade and then in Anderson's/Ramseur's/Cox's Brigade, Hill's/Rodes'/Grimes' Division, Army of Northern Virginia. Their service took them through every major and minor campaign associated with this great army, and they laid down their arms at Appomattox on April 9, 1865.

The flag of the 14th Regiment is of the 1st bunting type from the Richmond Depot, first issued in May 1862 to Longstreet's Corps. As a part of Colston's Brigade, the regiment likely received one of the first disbursements. These flags were 48" square, crossed by 8"-wide bars on which were sewn thirteen 3" cotton stars. The borders were orange bunting.

U.S. National Park Service, Gettysburg, Pa.

15th Regiment
North Carolina State Troops

This regiment was organized as the 5th Regiment North Carolina Volunteers and mustered into state service for twelve months at Garysburg, North Carolina, on June 11, 1861. In July, the regiment was assigned to the Department of the Peninsula in Virginia.

It was redesignated as the 15th Regiment North Carolina State Troops on November 14, 1861. As a part of Cobb's Brigade, the regiment took part in the Yorktown Siege of April-May 1862 and fought at the Battle of Lee's Mill on April 16, 1862. As a part of McGruder's command, the regiment may have been issued a battle flag used solely by this command. It was a white and red rectangular flag with the colors divided diagonally. If they were issued such a flag, it is not known to have survived the war.

In June of 1862, the Richmond Depot made a second wool issue of flags for the army. This differed from the first issue in that the width of the blue bars was lessened from 8" to 5". The orange border remained. The first flags went to D. H. Hill's division and a later issue was sent to the Department of the Peninsula.

The tattered remains of the regiment's 2nd wool issue battle flag are 45½" (hoist) x 39" (remains of fly). Six honors, three on each face, remain, as do two 3½" stars. The flag bears the War Department capture number 415 and is believed to have been captured during the Appomattox campaign.

Museum of the Confederacy, Richmond, Va.

16th Regiment
North Carolina State Troops

Organized for twelve months as the 6th Regiment North Carolina Volunteers at Raleigh on June 16, 1861, it was redesignated as the 16th Regiment North Carolina State Troops on November 14, 1861, and assigned to Gen. Wade Hampton's brigade.

This beautiful silk flag was created by one of Richmond's most artistic flag makers, Miss Rachel C. Seman. It is 39" (hoist) x 39" (fly). The field is of rose-colored silk and is crossed by 8"-wide blue silk bars forming a St. Andrew's cross. The cross is edged with 1"-wide white silk fimbriation. There are thirteen 2¾"-diameter white silk stars on the cross spaced at approximately 6½" centers. The stars are edged with small sequins and have one larger sequin centered in each star.

The unit name is embroidered in yellow silk thread in Roman uncial and miniscule letters; they are respectively 1⅝" and 1" high. The battle honors are embroidered in the same style, the letters being 1¾" and 1" high.

There are five pairs of white twill weave-braided ties, each ⅜" wide and 5" long. They are sewn to the ⅜"-wide twill weave-braid heading. The flag is edged with 2" deep gold fringe.

Although this flag is created in the style and material of the 1st (silk) Richmond issue, it is on record as having been presented to the regiment in 1863, likely very early in the year. It was carried by color-bearer Emanuel Rudisill of Gaston County. The flag was never captured and was carried home from Appomattox in the overcoat of a Colonel Stone.

North Carolina Museum of History, Raleigh, N.C.

EMANUEL RUDISILL

In 1861, at the age of 17, Emanuel Rudisill enlisted in Company M, 6th N.C.V. (later 16th N.C.S.T.). He became color bearer after a battle in which the regimental color bearer next to him was shot. Rudisill rescued the flag from the ground and rallied the surrounding troops to victory. Rudisill was officially promoted to ensign on August 17-18, 1864, and sustained wounds twice during his service as color bearer.

After the war, he moved to Texas, taking the flag with him and passing it down through his family as a treasured heirloom.

16th Regiment
North Carolina State Troops

This flag of the 16th Regiment North Carolina State Troops represents the unit's service from the Seven Days Campaign through Chancellorsville. The regiment received this Richmond Depot (3rd bunting issue) flag in June 1863 as a part of the general disbursement to A. P. Hill's Light Division.

It is 46½" (hoist) x 47" (fly). The red field is crossed with 5"-5¼"-wide blue bars forming a St. Andrew's cross. The cross is bordered with ½"-wide white cotton twill fimbriation. There are thirteen 3"-diameter cotton stars evenly spaced 6" apart. The unit designation is painted in yellow figures, the "16" being 1⅜" high and the "N.C." being 1½" high. The honors are in 1½" block letters painted blue (obverse only). Along the hoist edge is a 2"-wide canvas heading pierced with three whipped eyelets. The other three edges are bordered with 2"-wide white bunting.

The flag was captured by Pvt. Elijah M. Bacon of Company F, 14th Connecticut Infantry, at the battle of Gettysburg on July 3, 1863. For this act he was awarded the Congressional Medal of Honor. The flag is in relatively good condition, having been in service for only a month, save for the top right star being missing, possibly awarded to Private Bacon as a memento.

North Carolina Museum of History, Raleigh, N.C.

17th Regiment
North Carolina State Troops

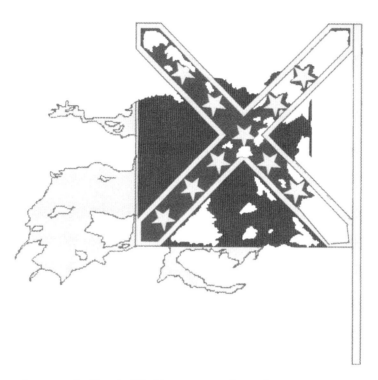

After its capture at Fort Hatteras and subsequent parole, the 17th Regiment North Carolina State Troops was organized a second time. The reborn regiment was organized at Camp Mangum on May 16, 1862, and mustered into Confederate service that same month. Its service in the Department of North Carolina took it through battles at Plymouth, Gardner's Bridge, Williamston, Tarboro, Foster's Mill, and Morehead City. In May 1864, the regiment, as a part of Martin's Brigade, was assigned to D. H. Hill's division, and served in Virginia at Bermuda Hundred, Fort Harrison, and the Petersburg siege. In December 1864, it was returned to North Carolina and assisted in the defense of Fort Fisher. It fought at the battle of Bentonville and surrendered at Durham Station on April 26, 1865.

There is little left of the 2nd National flag used by the 17th Regiment. The tattered remains are 55" along the hoist. The flag was hidden by Pvt. Able Thomas and taken home with him after the surrender.

North Carolina Museum of History, Raleigh, N.C.

18th Regiment
North Carolina State Troops

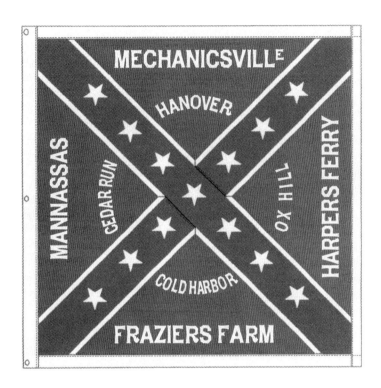

Organized for twelve months as the 8th Regiment North Carolina Volunteers at Camp Wyatt, near Wilmington, on July 20, 1861, the regiment was mustered into service there on August 20. In November, the regiment was redesignated 18th Regiment North Carolina State Troops.

Throughout 1862, the 18th Regiment, as a part of Branch's Brigade, saw service in every campaign associated with the Army of Northern Virginia from Seven Days to Fredericksburg. In December, Branch's/Lane's Brigade was issued colors marked with honors painted in white scalloped block letters. Every flag issued to the brigade in this distribution has survived, although that of the 7th Regiment is a small fragment of the original.

North Carolina Museum of History, Raleigh, N.C.

18th Regiment
North Carolina State Troops

In June 1863, Gen. A. P. Hill's Light Division received a disbursement of 3rd bunting issue flags from the Richmond Depot. The 18th Regiment North Carolina State Troops received the above flag at that time, shortly before leaving for the Pennsylvania campaign. The flag was carried at Gettysburg, Falling Waters, Bristoe Campaign, Mine Run, and the Wilderness in May 1864.

On May 11, 1864, General Lane's brigade defended the eastern line of defenses at Spottsylvania Courthouse, driving back assaults from General Burnside's IX Corps. On the following day, the brigade was moved closer to the angle at the north end of the line. While fighting raged to their left at the "muleshoe," Lane's Brigade once more found itself the target of Burnside's Corps.

Though assaulted by two divisions, Potter's and then Willcox's, the North Carolina Brigade held their line and resisted each charge thrown against them. Though successful in their defense of the line, the 18th Regiment lost a number of men captured along with the regimental colors.

The flag of the 18th Regiment was captured by Lt. A. H. Mitchell, Company A, 105th Pennsylvania Volunteers, on May 12, 1864. It was returned to the War Department and given capture number 118. The flag was returned to North Carolina in the general return of flags in 1905.

North Carolina Museum of History, Raleigh, N.C.

18th Regiment
North Carolina State Troops

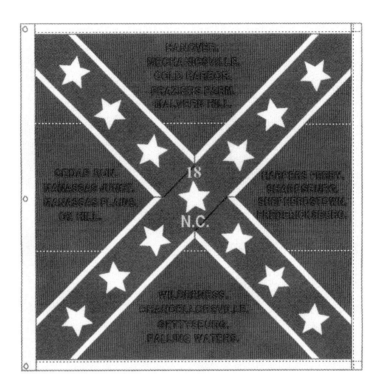

The 4th bunting issue of flags from the Richmond Depot was disbursed in the spring of 1864. Beginning in May, the 51" square flags were sent to the regiments. The 18th Regiment North Carolina State Troops received the above flag about that time. Peculiar to this design was the 8" spacing of stars giving the flag a more balanced look. The cross was formed of blue bars 6½"-7½" wide on which were sewn thirteen 5"-5½" white stars.

The above flag has 7"-wide bars displaying 5"-diameter stars. The hoist is 2" canvas pierced with three whipped eyelets. The other three edges are 1¾"-wide bunting. The honors are painted blue block letters and trace the regiment's service from Hanover (May 27, 1862) through Falling Waters (July 10, 1863).

This flag was captured on July 28, 1864, at Malvern Hill by Pvt. Timothy Conners, Company E., 1st U.S. Cavalry and given a War Department capture number of 150. It was returned to North Carolina in the general return of flags in 1905.

North Carolina Museum of History, Raleigh, N.C.

19th Regiment North Carolina State Troops
2nd Regiment North Carolina Cavalry

The 2nd Regiment North Carolina Cavalry was organized at Camp Clark, Kittrell's Springs, Granville County on August 30, 1861. First assigned to District of the Pamlico, Department of North Carolina, the regiment saw service in Ransom's Brigade and in W.H.F. Lee's Brigade, Cavalry Division, Army of Northern Virginia. They later served in Baker's/Gordon's/Barringer's Brigade.

Their engagements are too numerous to list but a notable few are Fredericksburg, Culpeper Court House, Manassas Junction, Wilderness, Petersburg, Hampton's Beef Steak Raid, and Dinwiddie Court House. The regiment was surrendered at Appomattox.

The flag of the 2nd Cavalry is a Richmond Depot 3rd (bunting) issue. It is 47" (hoist) x 48" (fly). The red field is crossed with 4½" blue bars edged with ½" white cotton fimbriation. Thirteen 3¼"-diameter white cotton stars are spaced at 6" intervals. The flag is bordered on three sides with 2" white edging and along the hoist with 1¾" canvas pierced with three whipped eyelets.

This flag was captured at Namozine Church, Virginia, April 1865, by Lt. Thomas W. Custer, 6th Michigan Cavalry.

Museum of the Confederacy, Richmond, Va.

Cabarrus Guards
Co. A, 20th Regiment North Carolina State Troops

Before sunup on Sunday, April 21, 1861, the sounds of fife and drum aroused the citizens of Concord, North Carolina. On this morning the Cabarrus Guards were boarding the trains and leaving their homes. Many of the townspeople marched with the boys to the depot. The Cabarrus Guards were wearing uniforms that one participant remembered as "the most attractive I have ever seen." Resplendent in "dark blue dress coats, with light blue pants, all belt trimmings white, and caps that were topped with red, white, and blue plumes" the company was among the finest offerings from the Old North State to the Southern war effort. "Each man looked full six feet tall with his plumes."

Leading the Cabarrus Guards was Capt. Nelson Slough, a veteran of the War with Mexico and a man who would gain fame as the commander of the 20th Regiment North Carolina State Troops.

The silk flag of the Cabarrus Guards is 28½" (hoist) x 40" (fly). The blue canton is 19" (hoist) x 18⅝" (fly). In modern times the frame holding the flag was apparently opened and the stars fell off. A shadow remains of a center star but the arrangement shown is hypothetical. The field is composed of red, white, and red bars, each one 9½" wide.

Cabarrus County Historical Society, Concord, N.C.

21st Regiment
North Carolina State Troops

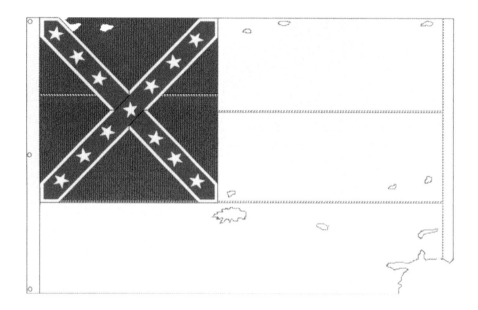

The 21st Regiment North Carolina State Troops was organized with twelve companies for twelve months as the 11th Regiment Volunteers at Danville, Virginia, on June 18, 1861. They were assigned to Milledge Bonham's brigade. They became the 21st Regiment North Carolina State Troops as a result of the reorganization of November 14, 1861. As a part of Trimble's/Hoke's brigade, the regiment saw action in the Shenandoah Campaign at Front Royal, 1st Winchester, and Cross Keys. As a part of the 2nd Corps, they participated in the Seven Days battles, Cedar Mountain, 2nd Manassas, and Chantilly.

Their service took them through every campaign of the Army of Northern Virginia, and they were surrendered at Appomattox on April 9, 1865.

The above 2nd National flag is 46" (hoist) x 71½" (fly). The canton is 30⅝" square. The red field is crossed by 3⅜"-wide blue bars edged with ½"-wide white cotton fimbriation. Thirteen 2¾"-diameter white cotton stars are evenly spaced on the St. Andrew's cross.

The flag was captured at Sayler's Creek, Virginia, in April 1865 by Pvt. William Shepherd, 3rd Indiana Cavalry.

Museum of the Confederacy, Richmond, Va.

22nd Regiment

North Carolina State Troops

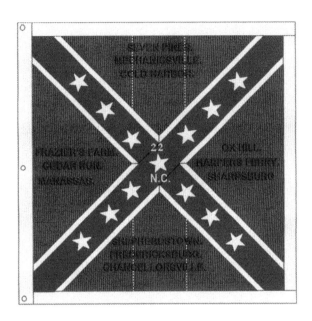

This regiment was organized with twelve companies as the 12th Regiment North Carolina Volunteers at Raleigh on July 11, 1861. Before the regiment was mustered in, Companies C and D became Companies A, 28th and A, 26th Infantry Regiments. It was mustered into Confederate service for twelve months during the summer of 1861, with Col. J. Johnston Pettigrew as its commander, and later redesignated 22nd Regiment North Carolina State Troops.

The regiment saw its first action at Evansport on December 9, 1861. As a part of Pettigrew's Brigade and later Pender's Brigade, the regiment saw action in the Seven Days battles, Cedar Mountain, 2nd Manassas, Sharpsburg, Fredericksburg, and Chancellorsville.

In late 1862 and early 1863, the Richmond depot issued the largest disbursement of battle flags. This disbursement is known as the 3rd issue. Gen. A. P. Hill's division, of which the 22nd was a member unit, received their flags in June 1863, just prior to leaving for Pennsylvania.

This 3rd issue Richmond Depot flag was captured by Pvt. Michael McDonough, 42nd N.Y. Volunteers, and given capture number 76. Other captures around this number are Gettysburg-related.

North Carolina Museum of History, Raleigh, N.C.

23rd Regiment
North Carolina State Troops

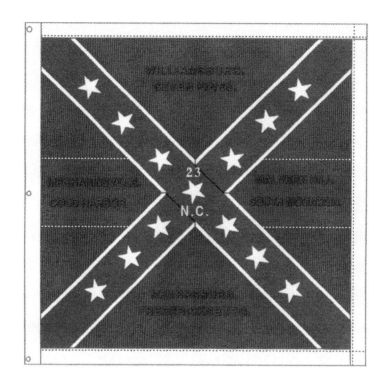

Organized as the 13th Regiment North Carolina Volunteers at Garysburg, North Carolina, on July 12, 1861, the unit was assigned to Early's Brigade, 1st Corps, Army of the Potomac. The regiment was mustered into state service for twelve months during the summer of 1861. In October it was placed in Van Dorn's Division of the 1st Corps. The regiment was redesignated as the 23rd Regiment North Carolina State Troops on November 14, 1861, and in February was assigned to D. H. Hill's Division, Army of Northern Virginia.

The service of the 23rd Regiment involves every campaign of the Army of Northern Virginia from the Siege of Yorktown in the spring of 1862 through the surrender at Appomattox.

This flag is a Richmond Depot 3rd (bunting) issue. It is 45" (hoist) x 46½" (fly). The red field is crossed by 5"-wide blue bars forming a St. Andrew's cross edged with ½" white cotton fimbriation. The white cotton stars are 3¼"-3½" diameter. The flag is edged on three sides with 2" white bunting and on the hoist with 2" white canvas pierced with three whipped eyelets. The honors are painted in blue block letters.

This flag was captured at Gettysburg on July 2, 1863, by the 2nd Division, 1st Army Corps.

North Carolina Museum of History, Raleigh, N.C.

EDWARD SCIPIO HART

"Ensign Edward S. Hart, of Company D, had been the color bearer of the 23rd Regiment on many previous occasions when he led the regiment at the Battle of Spottsylvania. "His character for gallantry in action was proverbial among his comrades." In this charge, he was knocked down "with the breach of a gun by a yankee," and he and the flag were captured. He is listed among the "Immortal Six Hundred," all Confederate officers held by Federals on Morris Island, Charleston harbor, as human shields in September and October 1864."

24th Regiment
North Carolina State Troops

This regiment was organized for twelve months as the 14th Regiment North Carolina Volunteers on July 18, 1861, and later redesignated 24th Regiment North Carolina State Troops. Their first assignment, from August to December of that year, was in the Army of the Kanawha. The regiment spent the winter at Petersburg, recovering from the West Virginia campaign. After a few months in the Department of Norfolk and in the Department of Northern Virginia, they were assigned to Ransom's Brigade, in which they saw action at Seven Days, Malvern Hill, Sharpsburg and Fredericksburg.

During Lee's Pennsylvania campaign, the 24th Regiment was assigned to protect the bridges for the return of the Army of Northern Virginia and saw action at Bottom's Bridge, July 4, 1863. The regiment participated in the recapture of Plymouth, North Carolina, on April 17-18, 1864. Returning to Virginia, they fought at Drewry's Bluff and Bermuda Hundred. At Weldon Railroad, on August 19, 1864, the above flag was captured by Pvt. George W. Reed, 11th Pennsylvania Volunteers.

It is 48" (hoist) x 48" (fly). The red field is crossed with 5"-wide blue bars, which are edged with ⅝" white cotton fimbriation. Eleven 3½" stars remain of the original thirteen. The remaining borders are 1⅞" white bunting. The hoist is 1⅞"-wide canvas pierced with three whipped eyelets.

North Carolina Museum of History, Raleigh, N.C.

24th Regiment
North Carolina State Troops

Under Gen. John B. Gordon, the 24th Regiment North Carolina State Troops fought in the desperate battle at Fort Stedman on March 25, 1865. Ransom's Brigade, on the left flank of the attack, moved forward and actually began to widen the gap in the Union defenses until the attack was halted by massive Union reinforcements. The 24th was engaged six days later at Dinwiddie Court House.

On April 1, 1865, at Five Forks, in what is called by some "the Waterloo of the Confederacy," the above flag was captured by Pvt. David Edwards, Company K, 146th New York Volunteers. A Richmond Depot 3rd bunting issue, it is 48" (hoist) x 50" (fly). The red field is crossed by 4½"-wide blue bars, which are edged with ¾"-wide white cotton fimbriation. Thirteen 3½"-diameter stars are spaced 6" on center. The flag is edged on three sides with 2"-wide white bunting, and on the hoist with 2"-wide canvas pierced with three whipped eyelets.

The flag was given a capture number of 275. It was returned to North Carolina along with the general return of 1905.

North Carolina Museum of History, Raleigh, N.C.

Cane Creek Rifles
Co. H, 25th Regiment North Carolina State Troops

This company, known as the "Cane Creek Rifles," was raised in Buncombe and Henderson counties and was enlisted in Henderson County on July 15, 1861. It was then mustered into state service and assigned to the 25th Regiment North Carolina State Troops.

The regiment was organized at Camp Clingman, near Asheville, on August 15, 1861, and spent the winter of 1861 in the Carolinas. In the spring of 1862, the regiment was attached to Ramseur's Brigade, and saw its first action in the Seven Days battles around Richmond. From this point, the 25th Regiment saw action in every major campaign of the Army of Northern Virginia, except Gettysburg. During the Pennsylvania campaign, the 25th was dispatched to guard the bridges that were important to Lee's return. The regiment was surrendered on April 9, 1865, at Appomattox Court House.

The flag of the Cane Creek Rifles is very tattered on the fly end. The flag was likely 44" square when new. The field is red bunting on which is embroidered a horn symbolic of the infantry in the War Between the States. Above the horn is embroidered the initials "C. C. R." Below the horn, in individual reverse-arched words, is "LIBERTY AND OUR NATIVE SOIL." The flag is edged on three sides with gold fringe. The reverse is white with the remains of a blue shield.

North Carolina Museum of History, Raleigh, N.C.

26th Regiment
North Carolina State Troops

The 26th Regiment North Carolina State Troops was organized at Crabtree, Wake County, on August 27, 1861. At its formation, Capt. Zebulon B. Vance of the 14th Regiment was elected its first colonel. Vance led the regiment for thirteen months during which the regiment distinguished itself at New Berne and in the Seven Days Campaign around Richmond. Colonel Vance was elected governor in 1862, taking office in September. Col. Henry K. ("Harry") Burgwyn assumed command of the regiment, leading the 26th through the New Berne and Washington campaigns of 1863 and to Gettysburg that summer.

One of the first units to reach Gettysburg, the 26th Regiment was thrown into battle on July 1, 1863, in the attack on Seminary Ridge. In this charge, color bearer after color bearer was shot down bearing this flag toward the enemy (see Appendix III). Nine in all fell in battle before the assistant inspector of the brigade took the colors and, waving them aloft, was instantly killed. The gallant "boy colonel," Burgwyn himself then reached for the colors and lifted them up when Pvt. Franklin L. Honneycut pleaded to be allowed to bear them. In handing the colors to the private, Burgwyn was shot through both lungs and, mortally wounded, fell to the ground. A moment later Honneycut was shot through the head.

The colors lay between the dying colonel and the dead private when Lt. Col. John R. Lane rode up. Though grief-stricken, he realized his new command,

and rode down the line to check his men. Upon returning, he saw the flag still on the ground and reached to pick it up. A lieutenant, upon seeing this action, cried out, "No man can take these colors and live!"

Calmly, and with a wave of his hand, Lane replied, "It is my time to take them now. Men of the 26th, follow me." A mighty shout answered the call and the regiment pressed forward and broke the last line that opposed its charge.

As Colonel Lane turned to see if his regiment was following, a Michigan rifleman took one last shot in parting. The ball crashed through Lane's neck and jaw. For the fourteenth time the colors were down. Lane was not expected to live, but the grit and determination of this brave man were underestimated. He survived to fight again and lived many years after the war.

This flag was found on the field at Gettysburg by the 12th New Jersey Infantry, returned to the U.S. War Department and given capture number 62. Unmarked, it was returned with the general return of 1905 to the Confederate Museum in Richmond.

This plain, unmarked flag is from the Richmond Depot's 3rd issue and is 45" (hoist) x 48½" (fly). The red field is crossed with 4½"-wide blue bars, which are edged with ½"-wide white fimbriation. There are thirteen 3½" white stars sewn at 6" centers. The flag is edged on three sides with 2" white bunting and is bordered on the hoist with 2" canvas pierced with three whipped eyelets.

Museum of the Confederacy, Richmond, Va.

26th Regiment
North Carolina State Troops

At the battle of Reams Station on August 25, 1864, the troops selected to carry the enemy's works were repeatedly driven back. General Heth's Division was ordered to their assistance. Arriving at his line, he sent a messenger back to procure a regimental flag. The messenger soon returned with color bearer Thomas Minton with the colors of the 26th Regiment North Carolina State Troops.

Wounded at Gettysburg, Minton had for some time been the color bearer for the 26th Regiment. Upon his arrival, Heth demanded the flag, intending as a gesture of leadership to lead the charge himself. Minton refused saying, "General, tell me where you want the flag to go and I will take it. I won't surrender up my colors."

Once more the general made his request and was rebuffed. "Come on then," Heth said to the stubbornly loyal bearer, "we will carry the colors together." With the flag waving right and left, the line advanced with a shout, through the abatis interlaced with wire, until Heth and Minton planted the flag on the enemy's breastworks.

This gallant color bearer was killed on October 27, 1864, at Burgess' Mill. These colors were finally taken from his hands by Sgt. Alonzo Smith, 7th Michigan Volunteers.

This 3rd bunting issue flag was issued to the regiment in September 1863 and led the regiment until its capture. It is 48" square and is very deteriorated, with most of the lower quarter missing.

North Carolina Museum of History, Raleigh, N.C.

Goldsboro Rifles
Co. A, 27th Regiment North Carolina State Troops

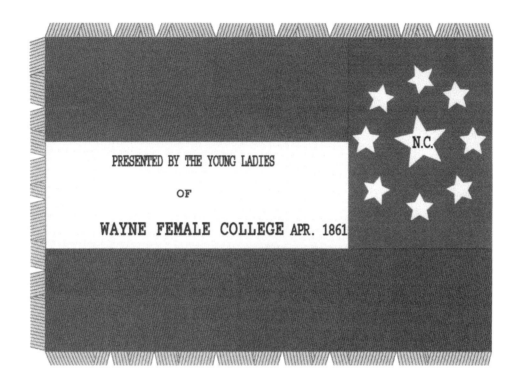

On March 18, 1886, a banquet celebration was held in Goldsboro. On this date, the above flag was returned to North Carolina by the 47th Massachusetts Regiment. Though severely tattered and shredded, this banner stirred the hearts of the members of the Goldsboro Rifles, still organized in defense of their state as Company D, 1st Regiment. North Carolina State Guard.

Twenty-five years earlier this flag was given to the Goldsboro Rifles by young ladies of Wayne Female College. This silk banner was created by Miss Requa's embroidery class and presented to the company prior to their service in the Confederate army. The flag was made in the first national style and measured 41½" (hoist) x 61" (fly). The canton measured 27⅝" (hoist) x 19½" (fly). In the blue canton, on the reverse, was a 6¾" star, in which was written "N.C.," and which was surrounded by eight 3⅝" stars. In the white center bar was embroidered, "PRESENTED BY THE YOUNG LADIES/OF/ WAYNE FEMALE COLLEGE, APR. 1861."

The front was similarly configured, except that on the white center bar was the unit designation and motto "GOLDSBORO RIFLES/VICTORY OR DEATH."

This company was raised in Wayne County and enlisted at Fort Macon in Carteret County on April 13, 1861. It was mustered into state service on June 13, 1861, and in September was mustered into Confederate service as Company A, 27th Regiment North Carolina State Troops. As a part of French's Brigade, the 27th Regiment saw action on March 18, 1862, in the defense of New Berne, North Carolina. The Union invasion, led by Gen. Ambrose Burnside, proved successful. In this battle, a Massachusetts regiment captured the flag of the Goldsboro Rifles. The men of Company A would not see their flag again for twenty-five years.

After New Berne, the regiment was sent to Virginia and participated in the Seven Days battle around Richmond and in every major campaign of the Army of Northern Virginia. The unit was surrendered at Appomattox on April 9, 1865.

North Carolina Museum of History, Raleigh, N.C.

In 1895, Furman Tudor (left) and Capt. Lewis D. Giddens of the Goldsboro Rifles posed with the flag of their Confederate predecessors.

Guilford Greys

Co. B, 27th Regiment North Carolina State Troops

The Guilford Greys were organized in Guilford County on October 15, 1860. Later they were incorporated into the 27th Regiment North Carolina State Troops as Company B.

This elaborate silk flag was presented to the company by a group of young ladies from Edgeworth Female Seminary in Greensboro at the coronation of their May queen, Mary Moorehead. The flag is 60" (hoist) x 70" (fly) and is bordered on three sides with 2"-wide gold fringe. Along the hoist are seven sets of ties. On the obverse is the state seal, the center line of which is 32½" from the hoist edge. Surrounding the seal is a wreath of ripened leaves.

A banner above the seal displays the company name in gold block letters shaded low and right in black. Below the wreath is a similar banner displaying in gold Roman uncial letters the date of organization. The reverse is a similar design save that the wreath is green; in the top banner is the phrase "E PLURIBUS UNUM." In the bottom banner is "GREENSBORO/N. CAROLINA." Within the wreath is a white field on which is written in gold "PRESENTED/by the/LADIES/OF EDGEWORTH/FEMALE/SEMINARY/May 5th, 1860."

Museum of the Confederacy, Richmond, Va.

Surry Regulators
Co. A, 28th Regiment North Carolina State Troops

This company, known as the "Surry Regulators" and the "Surry Marksmen," was raised in Surry County and enlisted at Dobson on May 4, 1861. It was originally assigned as Company C to the 22nd Regiment North Carolina State Troops but was withdrawn for some reason before the regiment was mustered in on July 11, 1861. The company was later assigned as Company A to the 28th Regiment North Carolina State Troops. The company functioned as part of this regiment for the duration of the war.

This silk flag of the Surry Regulators/Marksmen is 40" (hoist) x 86" (fly). The canton is 20" (hoist) x 23" (fly). This gives the flag an unusual configuration because the blue does not extend to the bottom of the white bar. Another flag, that of the Yadkin Gray Eagles, has a similar pattern. The flag of the Surry Marksmen is individualized, with the unit name embroidered in gold on the center white bar. The flag is edged on three sides with gold border. It was captured on March 11, 1861, at the Battle of New Berne by the 3rd New Jersey Regiment.

This flag is in poor condition, missing much material. The remains are extremely soiled, stained, and shattered.

North Carolina Museum of History, Raleigh, N.C.

28th Regiment
North Carolina State Troops

The 28th Regiment North Carolina State Troops was organized for twelve months at Camp Fisher, near High Point, on September 21, 1861. Under the command of Col. James H. Lane, the regiment was assigned to the Department of the Cape Fear through March 1862. In this command, they fought at the Battle of New Berne on March 14, 1862.

In March 1862, it was assigned to Branch's Brigade and served in this command throughout the war. The regiment arrived in Virginia in time to participate in the Battle of Hanover Court House on May 27, 1862.

This battle flag of the 28th Regiment is a Richmond Depot 3rd (bunting) issue. Flags of this type with honors painted in white were issued to Branch's North Carolina Brigade in December 1862. The flag is 48" (hoist) x 49" (fly). The red field is crossed by a St. Andrew's cross of 5"-wide blue bars edged with ¾"-wide white cotton fimbriation. The white cotton stars are 3½" diameter.

This flag was captured at the battle of Gettysburg in July 1863 by Capt. Morris Brown, Jr., 126th New York Infantry. It bears War Department capture number 66.

Museum of the Confederacy, Richmond, Va.

THE FLAGS OF CIVIL WAR NORTH CAROLINA

28th Regiment
North Carolina State Troops

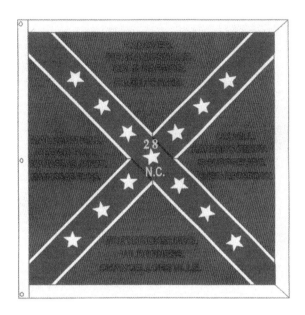

In June 1863, the regiments of A. P. Hill's Light Division were issued new flags from the Richmond Depot 3rd bunting issue. The 28th Regiment North Carolina State Troops received this flag during that disbursement and followed it through Gettysburg, Falling Waters, Bristoe, Mine Run, and the Wilderness. At the Battle of Spottsylvania, on May 11-12, 1864, Lane's Brigade fought with determined resolve, holding the eastern line against repeated assault. Though successful in its defense, there was considerable loss in the regiment. Among the casualties was this flag, captured by Cpl. John M. Kindig, Company A, 63rd Pennsylvania Infantry. It was returned to the War Department and given capture number 134.

It is 45½" (hoist) x 47½" (fly). The red bunting field is crossed with 4⅝"-wide blue bars edged with ⅝" white cotton fimbriation. Thirteen 3½"-diameter white cotton stars are sewn to the cross at 6" intervals. The flag is edged on three sides with 2" bunting and on the hoist with 2" canvas pierced with three whipped eyelets. The honors representing the regiment's service from May 1862 to May 1863 are painted in blue block uncial letters. The unit designation is painted in gold Roman uncial numerals and letters above and below the center star.

North Carolina Museum of History, Raleigh, N.C.

28th Regiment
North Carolina State Troops

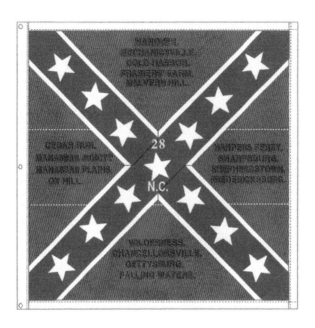

The Richmond Depot began the distribution of a 4th bunting issue in May 1864, due in part to the receipt of a number of boxes of bunting from England. The 28th Regiment North Carolina State Troops was issued this flag in time for the spring campaign beginning with the battle in the Wilderness. This flag was carried through Spottsylvania, North Anna, and Cold Harbor. On July 28, 1864, this flag was captured near Malvern Hill by Pvt. Samuel L. Malleck, Company I, 9th New York Cavalry. It was returned to the War Department and given capture number 149. Being only two months old at its capture, it is in relatively good shape with only a small portion of the lower hoist corner missing.

It is 50" (hoist) x 49" (fly). The field is crossed by 7"-wide blue bars, which are edged with ⅝"-wide white cotton fimbriation. Thirteen 5" stars are sewn to the cross at 8" intervals. The flag is edged on three sides with 1¾" white bunting and on the hoist with 1¾" canvas pierced with three whipped eyelets. The unit designation is painted in 1¾"-high Roman letters and numbers above and below the center star. The honors are painted in 1¼" blue block uncials.

North Carolina Museum of History, Raleigh, N.C.

28th Regiment
North Carolina State Troops

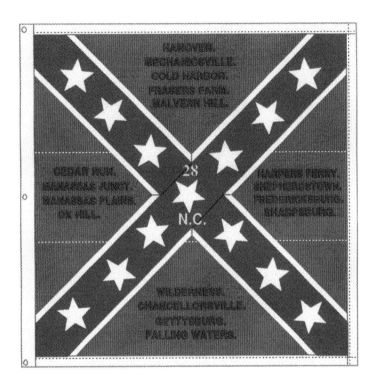

After the capture of its flag at Malvern Hill, the 28th Regiment North Carolina State Troops was issued a 4th bunting issue flag almost identical to the previous one. The main difference is in the order of honor placement in the fly quadrant. The flag was carried through the Petersburg Siege and battles at Reams' Station, Hatcher's Run, Battery Gregg, and Farmville. This flag was probably captured or surrendered at Appomattox on April 9, 1865. It was returned to the War Department and given capture number 364. It was returned to North Carolina with the general return of flags in 1905.

It is 49" (hoist) x 51½" (fly). The red field is crossed with 7" blue bars, which are edged with ¾" white cotton fimbriation. Thirteen 5" white cotton stars are sewn at 8" intervals to the cross. The unit designation is painted in gold above and below the center star and the honors are painted in blue block uncial letters. The flag is edged on three sides with 1½" white bunting and on the hoist with 2½" canvas pierced with three whipped eyelets.

North Carolina Museum of History, Raleigh, N.C.

29th Regiment
North Carolina State Troops

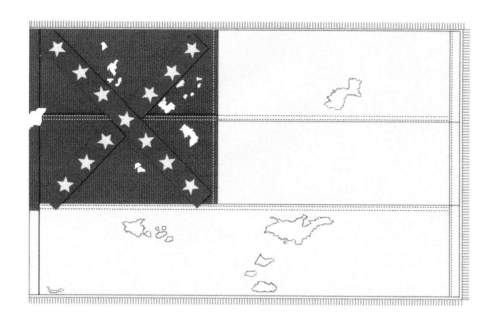

The 29th Regiment North Carolina State Troops was organized at Camp Patton near Asheville on September 24, 1861. This regiment saw service in many areas of the Western Theater, serving in the Army of Tennessee, the Department of Mississippi & East Louisiana, and the Department of Alabama, Mississippi & East Louisiana. Their service took them through most of the major campaigns associated with the Western army, including Murfreesboro, Chickamauga, the Atlanta Campaign, Franklin, and Nashville. In January 1865, the regiment was sent to help with the defense of Mobile, Alabama. This 2nd National flag was found after the evacuation of Spanish Fort in April 1865.

It is 51" (hoist, excluding fringe) x 85" (including hoist sleeve and excluding fringe). The canton is 32¼" (hoist) x 37½" (fly, including 1½" folded over to form a sleeve). The St. Andrew's cross is formed with one 4"-wide blue bar sewn over another. Thirteen 3"-diameter white cotton stars are spaced 6½"/13"/19" from center. The field is constructed of three panels of white bunting, which are, from top to bottom, 17½"/16"/17½". The flag is edged on three sides with 1½" white fringe.

Museum of the Confederacy, Richmond, Va.

30th Regiment
North Carolina State Troops

The 30th Regiment North Carolina State Troops was organized at Camp Mangum, near Raleigh, on September 26, 1861. The regiment was mustered into Confederate service for twelve months at Camp Lamb, Wilmington, on October 8, 1861. One company of the 20th Regiment was assigned as Company A, 30th Regiment, on this date. The regiment was reorganized for the war on May 1, 1862.

Shortly after its formation, the regiment was presented this regulation state flag. It is 55" (hoist) x approximately 80" (fly). The red field is 27" wide and is centered with a 20"-diameter white cotton star, oriented so that one point is directed toward the hoist. The dates prescribed by the 1861 Flag Act are embroidered above and below the star in white. The unit designation is embroidered at the bottom of the red field.

There is no record of this flag's capture.

North Carolina Museum of History, Raleigh, N.C.

30th Regiment
North Carolina State Troops

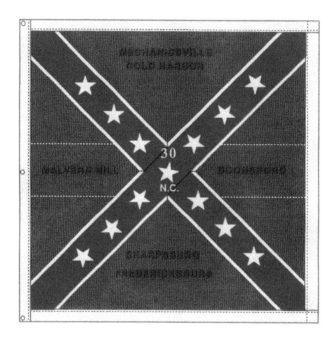

Traveling from North Carolina in the spring of 1862, the 30th Regiment North Carolina State Troops, with G. B. Anderson's Brigade, reached Virginia in time to participate in the Seven Days Campaign around Richmond. The regiment saw action at South Mountain, Sharpsburg, and Chancellorsville.

In April 1863, the regiments of D.H. Hill's Division received Richmond Depot 3rd (bunting) issue flags. This flag of the 30th Regiment is 47" (hoist) x 51" (fly). The red field is crossed with 5"-wide bars forming a St. Andrew's cross on which are thirteen 4"-diameter stars. The cross is edged with ½" white cotton fimbriation. The flag is bordered on three sides with 2" white bunting and on the hoist with 2"-wide canvas pierced with three whipped eyelets.

This flag was carried through Gettysburg, Bristoe, Mine Run, Kelly's Ford, Wilderness, and Spottsylvania, where on May 12, 1864, it was captured by Pvt. Robert W. Ammerman, Company B, 148th Pennsylvania Volunteers. The flag was sent to the War Department and given capture number 126.

The flag was returned to North Carolina along with the general return of flags, March 25, 1905.

North Carolina State Museum of History, Raleigh, N.C.

30th Regiment
North Carolina State Troops

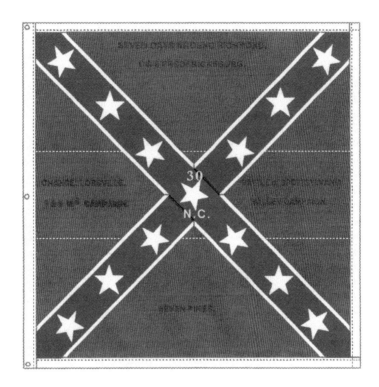

In June 1864, the 30th Regiment was part of Cox's Brigade, and served in the Valley District. In that year, they participated in battles at Lynchburg, Monocacy, Snicker's Gap, 3rd Winchester, Fisher's Hill, and Cedar Creek.

In September or early October, a fifth bunting issue was distributed from the Richmond Depot. Notable was a 9" span between stars. In the Valley an offshoot pattern was made at the Staunton Depot for those units of Wharton's Division that had lost their flags at Winchester. This flag of the 30th Regiment appears to be of the Staunton issue. It is 51" (hoist) x 51" (fly). The red field is crossed by 4⅞"-wide bars forming a St. Andrew's cross bearing thirteen 4½"-diameter stars on 9" centers. The cross is edged with ⅝"-wide white cotton fimbriation. The Staunton flags differed from the Richmond flags in that they were edged with 2"-wide white flannel instead of bunting.

There is no record of capture for this flag.

North Carolina State Museum of History, Raleigh, N.C.

O.K. Boys
Co. B, 31st Regiment North Carolina State Troops

This company was raised in Anson County and enlisted there on October 3, 1861, under the leadership of Capt. Edward R. Liles. It was then assigned to the 31st Regiment North Carolina State Troops and designated Company B.

This ornate flag was made by Tempie Liles and presented to the unit by the Ladies of Anson County. The field is composed of a white silk panel, 19" (hoist) x 41½" (fly), edged with 4¾"-wide gold brocade. On the central panel is the phrase "WOMEN.OF.ANSON./TO.THE/O.K. BOYS." painted in 1¾"-high gilt stylized Roman uncial letters. The flag is edged on three sides with ½"-wide blue silk to which is sewn 2" gold fringe attached with ¾" gold border.

The reverse of this flag is a Confederate 1st National. The canton is 20½" (hoist) x 21" (fly) upon which are eleven stars. The red/white/red field is composed of bars which are 10"/10"/10½", respectively, and displays the phrase "AUT VINCERE AUT MORT" (To Conquer or Die).

Captain Liles and this flag were captured February 8, 1862, at Roanoke Island by the 21st Massachusetts Infantry.

Museum of the Confederacy, Richmond, Va.

33rd Regiment
North Carolina State Troops

The 33rd Regiment North Carolina State Troops was organized in state service for the war at Raleigh in September 1861. The regiment, under its first commander, Colonel Lawrence O'Brian Branch (below), was attached to the District of the Pamlico, Department of North Carolina.

Transferred to Confederate service in January 1862, the regiment saw its first action two months later at the battle of New Berne. In May, it was transferred to the Army of Northern Virginia and on May 27 participated in the Battle of Hanover Courthouse.

This flag of the 33rd Regiment is a 1st National type with petal-like stars. It is 45" (hoist) x 69" (fly). The blue canton is 29" (hoist) x 27⅜" (fly). Eleven 5½"-diameter stars form a circle whose inner diameter is 13½". The flag is bound with ¾" twill ribbon. There is a ¾"-wide sleeve through which a rope passes for attachment to the staff.

North Carolina Museum of History, Raleigh, N.C.

33rd Regiment
North Carolina State Troops

This very decorative regimental marker flag was used by the 33rd Regiment North Carolina State Troops. The flag is entirely hand-sewn with metallic braid and fringe on the obverse only. The field of the flag is made of red silk. It is 16" (hoist) x 26" (fly). The edge is bordered on three sides with ½" decorative braid. Three-inch fringe decorates the fly end. There are button and tassel decorations on four corners. The button is 1½" diameter and the tassel is 6" long.

The unit designation is embroidered in white on the obverse only. The numbers are 3½" high. The "R" is 4" high and the "NC" is 3" high. The lower case "e" is 1½" high and the "g" is 3" high.

The flag's overall condition is listed as "fragile."

Museum of the Confederacy, Richmond, Va.

33rd Regiment
North Carolina State Troops

The 33rd Regiment North Carolina State Troops was organized in state service for the war at Raleigh in September 1861. At the time of formation, the regiment was presented this state flag. The regiment was assigned to the District of the Pamlico, Department of North Carolina, and on March 17, 1862, as a part of Gen. Lawrence O'B. Branch's Brigade, saw its first action at the Battle of New Berne. In this fight the above flag was captured.

It is 54" (hoist) x 80" (fly). The red field is 27" wide and centered with a 19"-diameter white cotton five-pointed star encircled by the two dates prescribed by the 1861 Flag Act. The unit designation is embroidered along the bottom of the red field which is of single-ply construction so that the inscriptions are in mirror-image on the flag's reverse.

North Carolina Museum of History, Raleigh, N.C.

JAMES W. ATKINSON
Color Bearer
33rd Regt., N.C.S.T.

James W. Atkinson, of Cumberland County, North Carolina, enlisted on March 1, 1862, at age 17. He was mustered in as a private.

Atkinson was wounded at or near Gaines Mill, Virginia, on or about June 27, 1862. He returned to duty prior to September 17, 1862, when he was wounded in both hands at Sharpsburg, Maryland. He returned to duty in November-December 1862 and was present or accounted for until he was wounded in the hip at Chancellorsville in early May 1863.

He was promoted to corporal August 1, 1863. He returned to duty prior to September 1, 1863, and was reduced in rank October 1, 1863. He was promoted to corporal in July-August 1863 and was present or accounted for until wounded while bearing the colors at Reams' Station, Virginia, on August 25, 1864. He returned to duty prior to September 30, 1864, when he was wounded in the leg at Jones' Farm, Virginia. He returned to duty in November-December 1864 and participated in the desperate defense of Fort Gregg, southwest of Petersburg, on April 2, 1865.

The battered Confederates were forced out of the defensive work after driving back six enemy assaults. Exhausted of ammunition, they resorted to throwing rocks and bricks but finally withdrew. Colonel Cowen of the 33rd Regiment wrote to Gen. James Lane, "Color Bearer James Atkinson made his escape from Fort Gregg after the enemy had entered it, and brought away the colors safely."

Lane attested to the heroism by adding, "I was an eye witness to the above. Atkinson ran from the fort when the enemy mounted the parapet, and with the colors of the Thirty-third North Carolina Regiment *flying*, he made his escape without being struck, though he was a marked target for the enemy. His exploit was greeted with cheers upon cheers from the men in the main line of works."

One week later, Atkinson surrendered with his regiment at Appomattox.

33rd Regiment
North Carolina State Troops

In June 1863, the regiments of Gen. A. P. Hill's Light Division were presented new flags from the Richmond Depot 3rd bunting issue. The unit designation in gold and the honors in blue block letters were common to this issue. The honors were applied in chronological order beginning with the top quadrant, then the hoist quadrant, fly quadrant, and lower quadrant. This flag shows the service of the 33rd Regiment North Carolina State Troops from March 17, 1862, through May 4, 1863. This flag was carried through Gettysburg, Falling Waters, Bristoe, Mine Run, and the Wilderness, where, on May 6, 1864, it was captured by 1st Sgt. J. Kemp, Company A, 5th Michigan Volunteers.

It is 46⅝" (hoist) x 48" (fly, remaining). The red field is crossed with 5" blue bars, which are edged with ½" white cotton fimbriation. Thirteen 3½"-diameter white stars are sewn to the cross at 6" centers. The flag is edged on the top and bottom (the fly edge is tattered and missing) with 1½" white bunting and on the hoist with 1½" canvas pierced with three whipped eyelets.

North Carolina Museum of History, Raleigh, N.C.

34th Regiment
North Carolina State Troops

The 34th Regiment North Carolina State Troops was organized on October 25, 1861.

This flag of the 34th Regiment is a 1st National variation. It is 46" (hoist) x 72" (fly). The blue canton is 30⅝" (high) x 31¼" (wide). Thirteen 4"-diameter white cotton stars are sewn to the canton in a pattern that represents the Ark of the Covenant. The bottom eight stars represent the box in which the Ten Commandments were kept. The right and left pairs of stars represent the angels guarding the Ark, and the center star represents God's presence (the Shekinah). Other flags displaying this pattern are the Phillips (Georgia) Legion (in the National Park Service collection) and the headquarters flag of Gen. Robert E. Lee (at the Museum of the Confederacy).

The number "420" is stenciled on the center bar signifying its capture. The date of capture is not known, although the number itself is among others captured at Appomattox. The flag was returned to North Carolina on March 25, 1905.

North Carolina Museum of History, Raleigh, N.C.

34th Regiment
North Carolina State Troops

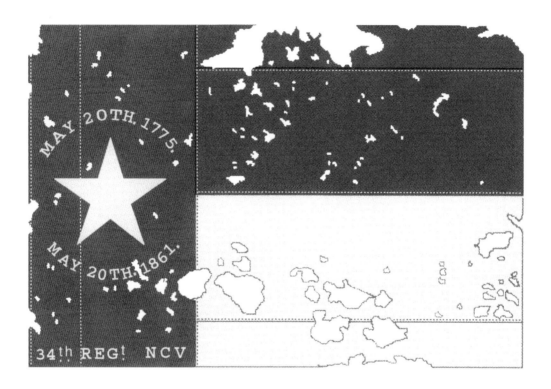

This state flag was presented to the 34th Regiment North Carolina State Troops shortly after its organization on October 25, 1861. It was captured by the 2nd Regiment New Hampshire Volunteers and left in the hands of Capt. George H. Colby of that regiment.

The flag is 54" (hoist) x 82" (fly). The red bunting field is 26¾" wide. Centered on the red field is a 20"-diameter white cotton five-pointed star. Encircling the star are the two dates prescribed by the Flag Act of 1861. Along the lower edge of the red field is the unit designation, "34th REG'T N.C.V." The dates and unit designation are embroidered in white on the single-ply red field so that on the reverse the characters are seen in mirror image.

This flag is in very deteriorated condition.

North Carolina Museum of History, Raleigh, N.C.

34th Regiment
North Carolina State Troops

In June 1863, Gen. A. P. Hill's Division, soon to be Gen. Dorsey Pender's Division, was presented flags of the Richmond Depot's 3rd bunting issue. The 34th Regiment North Carolina State Troops received this flag, which was then carried on the Pennsylvania campaign and at the battle at Gettysburg, Pennsylvania.

At camp near Bunker Hill, Virginia, after Gettysburg, on July 17, Lt. Burwell Thomas, Company K, 34th Regiment, wrote his sister:

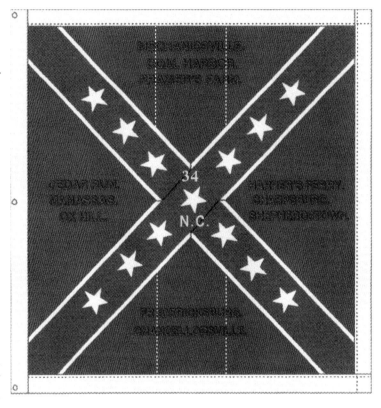

"We routed the yankees on the 1st and drove them back about two miles and then stopped and let them fortify and charged them through an open field 1½ miles to their breast works. They threw shells, grape and canister as thick as hail. When we got in two hundred yards of them the infantry opened on us but onward we pressed until more than two thirds of the troops had been killed, wounded and straggled. Our lines were broken and we commenced retreating. A good many surrendered rather than risk getting out. They captured four flags in our brigade leaving only one."

This flag of the 34th Regiment was among those captured at Gettysburg. It is 47" (hoist) x 46" (fly). The red field is crossed with 5"-wide blue bars, which are edged with ½" white fimbriation. The flag is edged on three sides with 2" white bunting and on the hoist with 2" canvas pierced with three whipped eyelets.

North Carolina Museum of History, Raleigh, N.C.

35th Regiment
North Carolina State Troops

The 35th Regiment North Carolina State Troops was organized at Camp Mangum, near Raleigh, on November 8, 1861, around which time the above flag was presented. The regiment was assigned first to the District of the Pamlico, Department of North Carolina, and fought at New Berne in March 1862.

In April 1862, the regiment was attached to Ransom's Brigade, and accompanied the brigade to Virginia. In this command, the 35th saw action at Seven Days and all further campaigns associated with the Army of Northern Virginia, except Gettysburg. During Lee's Pennsylvania campaign, the 35th was assigned to protect the bridges important to the return of the Army of Northern Virginia. The 35th North Carolina was surrendered at Appomattox on April 9, 1865.

This state issue flag is 51" (hoist) x 68" (fly). The red field is centered with a 17½" white star, above and below which are embroidered the dates as called for in the 1861 Flag Act.

This flag was captured at Petersburg on June 17, 1864, by Cpl. Young, Company I, 1st Michigan Infantry.

North Carolina Museum of History, Raleigh, N.C.

35th Regiment
North Carolina State Troops

This machine-stitched flag of the 35th Regiment North Carolina State Troops is a Richmond Depot 4th bunting issue and was delivered to the regiment in the summer of 1864.

It is 48" (hoist) x 50" (fly). The red field is composed of three horizontal bunting panels, which are 18"/14"/17" wide, respectively. The field is crossed with 6½"-wide blue bars, which are edged with ½" white cotton fimbriation. Thirteen 5"-diameter white polished cotton stars are sewn to the cross. The stars are spaced on 7½" centers. The flag is bordered on three sides with 1¾"-wide white bunting and along the hoist with a 2¼"-wide canvas heading, which is pierced with three whipped eyelets.

At some point two pairs of twill tape ties were hand-sewn to the hoist edge, between the whipped eyelets. One pair has a red and a blue tie, measuring 10". The other pair has a remnant of the red tie and a 10" piece of blue attached. One piece of white twill tape is looped through the center eyelet.

This flag was captured at the battle of Five Forks, Virginia, in April 1865 by Lt. Henry G. Bonebrake, 17th Pennsylvania Cavalry. It was returned to the War Department and given capture number 340.

Museum of the Confederacy, Richmond, Va.

Kennedy Light Artillery

Co. G (2nd), 36th North Carolina State Troops
Co. G (2nd), 2nd North Carolina Artillery Regiment

This company was organized in Beaufort County on September 23, 1861, and reorganized for three years or the duration of the war on April 21, 1862. The company was assigned to the 2nd Regiment North Carolina Artillery on May 12, 1862, with Zachariah T. Adams as captain. On November 4, 1863, the battery became Company D, 13th Light Artillery Battalion.

This battery was attached to the Department of North Carolina and Southern Virginia, and saw action at Washington and New Berne. In 1864, it was stationed at Kinston. Later the company was at Batteries Purdie and Bolles near Fort Fisher. On January 15, 1865, most of the company and all its guns and horses were captured. The few remaining men were attached to General Hagood's Brigade, fought at Bentonville, and were surrendered with the Army of Tennessee.

The blue silk flag of the Kennedy Light Artillery is 40" square and is edged on three sides with 3" white metallic fringe. The letters are 5", the stars are 6", and the flag was attached to the staff with four sets of blue ties. It was never lost or surrendered.

North Carolina Museum of History, Raleigh, N.C.

Pvt. Kit Bland at the Battle of Fort Fisher

During the bombardment of Fort Fisher, December 1864, Private Kit Bland, 36th Regiment, made himself one of the heroes of the war when the Confederate flag was shot away and dangled from its high staff above the fort. Bland, like Sargeant Jasper in the Revolutionary War, climbed the staff and refastened the flag, only to see it struck by another shot. Again he shinnied his way up the pole and with his necktie fastened the flag so securely that it remained aloft throughout the remainder of the intense bombardment.

Gaston Blues
Co. H, 37th Regiment North Carolina State Troops

This company, known as the "Gaston Blues," was raised in Gaston County and was enlisted at Dallas on October 6, 1861. It was mustered into state service on November 20, 1861, and was assigned to the 37th Regiment North Carolina State Troops as Company H.

According to tradition, women converted their gowns into this company flag for the Gaston Blues. According to one source, the flag was "captured by Federals" and "later returned to North Carolina." It is not, however, in the Museum of North Carolina History or the Gaston County Museum of History in Dallas. It was once reported in the 1950s, but not documented, to have been in a private collection in upstate New York. It is still missing. This illustration was taken from a black and white photograph of the flag printed in *North Carolina Illustrated.* The flag is a 1st National design with stars arranged in radial symmetry. "GASTON BLUES" is line-stitched onto the white bar, as is the smaller date, "1861."

Location unknown

37th Regiment
North Carolina State Troops

The 37th Regiment North Carolina State Troops was organized at High Point on November 20, 1861. Under its first commander, the regiment saw action at the Battle of New Berne on March 18, 1862. After reorganization in April 1862, the regiment, as a part of Branch's Brigade, traveled to Virginia. In Branch's (later Lane's) Brigade, the 37th North Carolina took part in every major campaign of the Army of Northern Virginia and was surrendered at Appomattox on April 9, 1865.

This 47½" square Richmond Depot 3rd issue flag represents one of the earliest types issued to the regiments of the Army of Northern Virginia. Branch's Brigade received these flags, distinctive for their honors painted in large white scalloped letters, in December 1862. In addition to the honors illustrated, on the reverse are honors for MANASSAS JUNCTION, SHARPSBURG, MECHANICSVILLE, HARPERS FERRY, and SHEPERDS-TOWN. Remarkably, all of these similarly marked flags of Branch's Brigade have survived, although that of the 7th Regiment is in fragmentary form.

This flag was captured near Petersburg, Virginia, in April 1865 by Cpl. Richard Welch, 37th Massachusetts Infantry. It was given capture number 384.

For many years after its return in 1905 this flag was displayed in the Lee Chapel at Washington & Lee University.

Museum of the Confederacy, Richmond, Va.

38th Regiment
North Carolina State Troops

The 38th Regiment North Carolina State Troops was organized for twelve months at Camp Mangum, near Raleigh, on January 17, 1862. In April, it was reorganized for the war and received this Raleigh Clothing Depot state battle flag. It is 54" (hoist) x 80" (fly). The red field is 26¾" wide and is centered with a 19"-diameter white cotton star. Above and below the star, embroidered in white, are the two dates prescribed by the 1861 Flag Act. The unit designation is embroidered along the lower edge of the red field. The blue and white bars are each 27" wide.

Attached to Pender's Brigade, the regiment saw action in the Seven Days Campaign, June 1862, and participated in every subsequent campaign of Lee's Army of Northern Virginia, laying down arms at Appomattox.

This flag has no record of capture and was likely brought home to North Carolina after the war.

North Carolina Museum of History, Raleigh, N.C.

38th Regiment
North Carolina State Troops

For the first two months after its organization, the 38th Regiment North Carolina State Troops was assigned to the Department of North Carolina, and in March was placed under the command of Brig. Gen. J. R. Anderson. In June 1862, the regiment became a part of Dorsey Pender's Brigade and in this capacity served throughout the war.

The regiment's first action was in the Seven Days Campaign. At Mechanicsville on June 26, 1862, the 38th advanced to outflank entrenched Federal artillery and infantry, losing nearly one-third of its number. The wounded color bearer remained at the regiment's head and brought this 2nd bunting issue flag to safety.

This flag is 48" (hoist) x 47" (fly). The red field is crossed by 5"-wide blue bars edged with ½"-wide white cotton fimbriation. The thirteen stars are 3½" in diameter. "38/NC" is painted in gold on the lower quadrant. The flag is bordered on three sides with 1½"-wide orange bunting. Along the hoist is a white canvas heading with three whipped eyelets.

North Carolina State Museum, Raleigh, N.C.

38th Regiment
North Carolina State Troops

After the Seven Days Campaign, and as a part of Gen. Dorsey Pender's Brigade, the 38th Regiment North Carolina State Troops saw action at Cedar Mountain, 2nd Manassas, Harper's Ferry, Fredericksburg, and Chancellorsville. With Pender promoted to division command, Brig. Gen. Scales led the 38th Regiment to Gettysburg. In the initial assault of July 1st, the regiment *"encountered a most terrific fire of grape and musketry in front."* Lt. Col. George Flowers remembered that *"every officer in Scales' Brigade except one, Lieutenant Gardman, upon whom the command devolved, was dis-*

abled, 400 men killed, wounded and missing," one-fourth of whom were from the 38th Regiment.

Colonel Lawrence took command of the brigade, and Captain Thornburg of the regiment. On July 3, the regiment was placed on the far right of the attack and *"ordered forward over a crimson plain."* They made it to within *"a few feet of the enemy's line,"* but at a terrible cost. Every man in Company A, except two who were captured, was shot down. *"After the third day's fight the regiment had only about forty men, commanded by a first lieutenant."*

This tattered flag, 47" square, was captured at Gettysburg on the third day's assault by Sgt. George H. Dore, 126th New York Infantry. It is a 3rd bunting issue with 4¾" blue bars bordered with ½" fimbriation, thirteen 3⅜" stars, 1½" white bunting borders, and 1½" canvas hoist.

Museum of the Confederacy, Richmond, Va.

38th Regiment
North Carolina State Troops

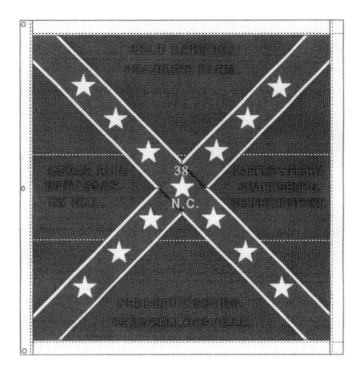

In June 1863, the 38th Regiment North Carolina State Troops was presented this Richmond Depot flag. The flag, of the 3rd bunting issue, is 46" square. It is crossed with 4½"-wide blue bars forming a St. Andrew's cross, which is edged with ½" white cotton fimbriation. The stars, 3½" in diameter, are spaced 6" apart. Three edges are bordered with 2" white bunting while the hoist edge is 1¾" canvas pierced with three whipped eyelets. The unit designation is painted in gold above and below the center star. Honors painted in blue block letters show the regiment's service from the Seven Days Campaign through the spring of 1863. This flag was carried by the regiment for the duration of the war and, with a capture number of 400, was likely captured or surrendered at Appomattox. The flag is quite tattered, particularly along the fly.

This flag was returned to North Carolina along with the general return of flags from the U.S. War Department on March 25, 1905.

North Carolina Museum of History, Raleigh, N.C.

Highland Grays

Co. D, 39th Regiment North Carolina State Troops

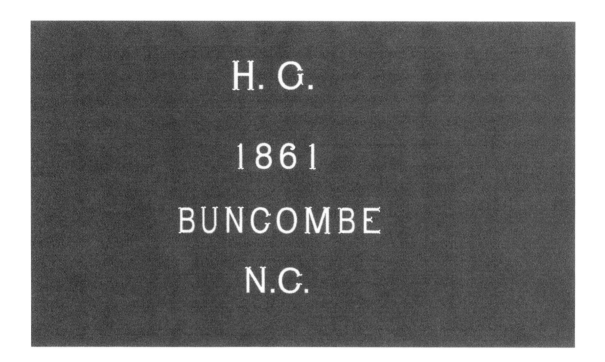

The mountains of North Carolina have long been called the "Highlands," not merely because of their heights but because of the large number of Highland Scots who found their way to the region after leaving the Old Country. Rather than displace the native Cherokee, these incoming Scots shared the mountains with the Indians, becoming trading partners, friends, and at times, family, through intermarriage.

At the outbreak of war, these two groups became allies for the Southern cause, as the above flag illustrates. The Bowie knife, brandished by a strong arm coming from a red and white base shows the combined heritage of the Highland Grays. This force of Cherokee and Scottish southerners would, if the Latin phrase *"DIRIGAT DEUS"* may be loosely translated, "wreak destruction on their enemy for as long as it took for victory to be obtained."

The company known as the "Highland Grays" was raised in Buncombe County and was enlisted at Asheville on October 28, 1861. It was then ordered to Camp Patton, Asheville, and was designated Company D of Maj. David Coleman's Battalion, North Carolina Troops, when that unit was organized on December 10, 1861.

When the battalion was reorganized as a regiment on May 19, 1862, the company became Company D, 39th Regiment North Carolina State Troops. The first company commander was Capt. Ambrose Gaines. Capt. Allen Williams led the company as part of the 39th Regiment. The company records show a sad note in that at the end of the war, Captain Williams was "murdered at his farm by plunderers."

The blue silk flag of the Highland Grays is 40" (hoist) x 68" (fly). On the obverse is embroidered "H.G./N.C./BUMCOMBE/1861." The letters forming "H.G." are $3\frac{3}{8}$" high while the rest are $3\frac{1}{4}$". On the reverse is a design, reminiscent of early pirate flags, showing a strong arm brandishing a Bowie knife, above which is embroidered in $3\frac{1}{3}$"-high letters the Latin phrase "DIRIGAT DEUS."

North Carolina Museum of History, Raleigh, N.C.

39th Regiment
North Carolina State Troops

In January 1862, at Reem's Creek, two companies, F and G, were added to Coleman's Battalion. Later, a company from Cherokee County joined the battalion as Company H. The battalion was moved to Knoxville, Tennessee, and on May 19, 1862, after picking up a company from Macon County, was redesignated the 39th Regiment North Carolina State Troops.

Before the regiment left for Tennessee, a group of ladies from Asheville presented this flag to the unit. This 52" (hoist) x 62" (fly) blue banner with its 3½"-wide white cross is a true flag of St. Andrew, save for the 15" x 15" x 22" red triangles representing the Cherokee contingency of the command. The heading is a ⅞"-wide white cotton hoist with seven whipped eyelets.

This flag is the earliest of a line of flags associated with Gen. John P. McCown's Division. When the 39th North Carolina was sent to east Tennessee, it was not immediately attached to a specific command. When McCown, himself of Scottish ancestry, was transferred to the department, he could not help but notice the 39th flag. He chose the design, without the triangles, to represent his command.

The flag was carried by the 39th through severe fighting at Murfreesboro and Chickamauga and is in very tattered condition.

North Carolina Museum of History, Raleigh, N.C.

39th Regiment
North Carolina State Troops

This Department of Alabama, Mississippi, and East Louisiana battle flag reflects the western service of the 39th Regiment North Carolina State Troops. At Murfreesboro, the 39th Regiment took part in the capture of enemy artillery during the fight on December 31. They served at the siege of Jackson, Mississippi. At Chickamauga, the 39th Regiment *"already in advance of the line, charged furiously upon the batteries diagonally on the right and captured them, taking ten pieces. . . ."*

This gallant act of the 39th is remembered in the motto: "Farthest to the Front at Chickamauga." The regiment went on to see action during the Atlanta Campaign and fought at Franklin and Nashville. Their last action was in defense of Mobile Bay at Spanish Fort, where the above flag was captured.

The flag is 45½" (hoist) x 49" (fly, including the hoist). The blue bars are 8" wide and are edged with 1¼" white cotton fimbriation. The twelve stars are 4" in diameter. The Roman letters are cut from white cotton and are 2" high.

North Carolina Museum of History, Raleigh, N.C.

40th Regiment North Carolina State Troops

3rd Regiment North Carolina Artillery

The organization of this regiment began in January 1862, but was first completed at Fort Holmes, Smith's Island, on December 1, 1863. The individual companies of this regiment saw action at forts Anderson and Fisher and during the Carolinas Campaign of 1865. Most of the companies fought their last battle at Bentonville, North Carolina, March 19-21, 1865.

This silk flag of the 40th Regiment North Carolina State Troops is a hand-sewn Army of Northern Virginia variant. It is 22½" (hoist) x 21⅝" (fly). Thirteen 3³⁄₁₆" white stars are sewn to 3¾" blue bars, which are edged with ⅛"-wide fimbriation. The blue bars are sewn to the red silk field, one crossing over the other. The silk is in very tattered condition.

North Carolina Museum of History, Raleigh, N.C.

41st Regiment North Carolina State Troops

3rd Regiment North Carolina Cavalry

The 41st Regiment North Carolina State Troops/3rd Regiment North Carolina Cavalry was organized in the field beginning on September 3, 1862. Organization was completed on August 18, 1863. From September 1862 through July 1863, the regiment served in the Department of North Carolina and saw action at Washington (North Carolina) and Jamesville, and participated in the capture of the *U.S.S. Ellis.*

In the spring of 1863, the regiment was attached to the Department of North Carolina and Southern Virginia and saw action at South Anna Bridge on July 4, 1863. After July 1863, the 3rd Cavalry served in Virginia as part of the Department of Richmond and later in Barringer's Brigade of the Army of Northern Virginia. In this capacity it participated in many battles associated with that great army, including the Petersburg Siege, Reams' Station, and the Hampton Beefsteak Raid. The 3rd Cavalry was surrendered at Appomattox on April 9, 1865.

This flag is a Richmond Depot 3rd (bunting) issue flag and is 45⅝" (hoist) x 44" (fly, remaining). The red field is crossed with 4¾" blue bars forming a St. Andrew's cross, which is edged with ⅝" fimbriation. There were thirteen 3½" white cotton stars, one of which is missing along with a large part of the lower fly corner. Along the top and bottom are the remains of 1⅞-2" white edging. The hoist is edged with 2"-wide canvas, which is pierced with three whipped eyelets.

North Carolina Museum of History, Raleigh, N.C.

42nd Regiment
North Carolina State Troops

The 42nd Regiment North Carolina State Troops was organized in Salisbury on April 22, 1862, and commanded by Col. George C. Gibbs. Assigned to the Department of North Carolina, the regiment served at Weldon as railroad security to the Wilmington/Weldon Railroad, the "lifeline of the Confederacy." Some time after May 1863, while in Martin's Brigade, Department of North Carolina, the regiment was issued this 2nd National flag.

It is 73" (hoist) x 107" (fly). The white field is composed of four 18¼"-wide horizontal panels. The canton is 45" (hoist) x 48" (fly) and is crossed with 5⅜" blue bars, which are edged and wrapped on the ends with ½" white fimbriation. Thirteen 4⅜"-diameter white cotton stars are sewn to the cross. Along the hoist is a 1½"-wide canvas sleeve.

North Carolina Museum of History, Raleigh, N.C.

42nd Regiment
North Carolina State Troops

As a part of Martin's Brigade, the 42nd Regiment North Carolina State Troops traveled to Virginia in 1864 and participated in the campaign at Bermuda Hundred in May and June of that year. The regiment fought at Cold Harbor, the Petersburg Siege, Fort Harrison in September, and Burgess' Mill on October 27, 1864. Returning to North Carolina, the regiment participated in both Fort Fisher battles and was surrendered at Durham Station on April 26, 1865.

This machine-sewn flag is of the Richmond Depot 4th bunting issue. This issue was distributed beginning in May 1864, about the time the 42nd Regiment arrived in Virginia. It is 48" (hoist) x 51" (fly). The red field is crossed with 4⅝"-wide blue bars, which are edged with ½" white cotton fimbriation. Thirteen 4" stars are sewn to the cross. The flag is bordered on three sides with 1½" white bunting and on the hoist with 2"-wide canvas heading pierced with three whipped eyelets. The unit designation has been appliqued to the flag in the hoist and fly quadrants.

North Carolina Museum of History, Raleigh, N.C.

44th Regiment
North Carolina State Troops

The 44th Regiment North Carolina State Troops was organized at Camp Mangum, near Raleigh on March 28, 1862, with George B. Singletary as its colonel. On May 19, 1862, the regiment was ordered to Tarboro, North Carolina. From there it went to Greenville, North Carolina, and for a few weeks was engaged in outpost and picket duty in that area of the state.

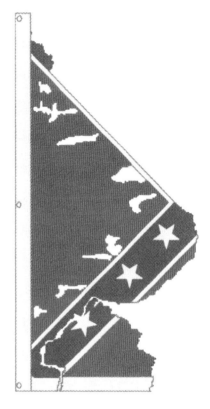

From eastern North Carolina, the regiment was ordered to Virginia and there assigned to the brigade of Gen. J. Johnson Pettigrew. In this brigade the 44th saw action in almost every engagement of the Army of Northern Virginia. One notable exception was Gettysburg. En route to Pennsylvania, the 44th was detached from the brigade to guard the bridges at Hanover Junction. On June 26th, the 44th Regiment North Carolina State Troops engaged in an unbelievably stubborn defense of these bridges against a Union cavalry force of 1,500 men. The fight conducted by Lieutenant Colonel Hargrove and his grossly outnumbered men was successful and is remembered as one of the noblest defenses of the war.

The regiment served with the Army of Northern Virginia until the end. The first flag issued to the 44th Regiment was carried throughout the war, until around January 1, 1865, when a new one was issued. So much of the old flag had been shot away that it could not be distinctly seen by other regiments during brigade drill.

"The old battle flag of the regiment, tattered and torn by ball and shell, its staff riddled and its folds in shreds, was presented to Mrs. Della Worth Bingham, wife of Captain Robert Bingham, Co. G [pictured below] by the Major commanding, as a mark of respect and esteem in behalf of officers and men to a woman who had won their affectionate regard, and whose husband had ever followed it with fidelity and fortitude upon every field where it waved. Captain Bingham, whose home is in Asheville, N.C. still has it in his possession."

Southern Historical Society Papers, Vol. XXV, Jan-Dec. 1897, p. 345

The flag of the 44th Regiment was a Richmond Depot 3rd bunting issue flag. The larger remnant of the flag shows 4½" blue bars edged with ½" white fimbriation. Two 3½"-diameter stars remain. The hoist is 45".

The smaller fragment is at the Museum of the Confederacy. This remnant was presented to the museum by color bearer Pvt. William S. Long, who carried it from Fredericksburg to Appomattox.

The new battle flag was carried by color bearer Sgt. George Barber of Company G until the night of April 1, 1865, when crossing the Appomattox, he wrapped it around a stone and dropped it in the river, saying to his comrades about him, *"No enemy can ever have a flag of the 44th North Carolina Regiment."*

Private collection/Museum of the Confederacy, Richmond, Va.

The Flag of the 45th Regiment
North Carolina State Troops

"I send to you the flag of the 45th N.C. Troops, which the members of the Regt. desire your Excellency to have placed among the archives of our dear old State which we love the more the longer this inhuman and unnatural war continues. We have endeavored to take care of our flag, but it is much tattered and torn—a fair representative of the service this Regt. has seen. The staff has been shot nearly off three or four times. At Gettysburg, two Color bearers were killed and all the Color Guard killed or wounded. Our losses around these colors since that battle have been fearful."

Letter from Col. John R. Winston, 45th Regt. N.C.S.T.,
to Gov. Zebulon B. Vance

(current location of flag not known)

46th Regiment
North Carolina State Troops

The 46th Regiment North Carolina State Troops was organized at Camp Mangum, near Raleigh, in April 1862. Assigned to Walker's (later Cooke's) Brigade, the regiment saw its first action in the Seven Days battles around Richmond. Though the regiment saw service in the Department of North Carolina and the Department of South Carolina, Georgia, and Florida, its primary service was with General Lee's Army of Northern Virginia, participating in all the major campaigns of this command. The regiment was surrendered at Appomattox on April 9, 1865.

All that is left of the 46th Regiment's state flag is a portion of the red field, the remains of which are 52" high. The characters are embroidered in satin stitch.

It was picked up on the picket line at Petersburg, Virginia., by Lt. William Brant, Jr., Company B, 1st New Jersey Volunteers and given capture number 342. The flag was returned to North Carolina in 1905.

North Carolina Museum of History, Raleigh, N.C.

47th Regiment
North Carolina State Troops

The 47th Regiment North Carolina State Troops was organized on April 9, 1862, and was assigned to Ransom's Brigade, Department of North Carolina. From the Seven Days battles through Appomattox, the 47th Regiment saw service in all the major campaigns of the Army of Northern Virginia. The above North Carolina State flag was presented to the regiment at its formation and was carried with the unit until April 2, 1865, when it was captured by Pvt. Joseph Phillips, Company E, 148th Pennsylvania Volunteers, at Sutherland Station, Virginia. It was given capture number 354.

The 47th Regiment was surrendered at Appomattox on April 9, 1865.

This flag is 53" (hoist) x 65¾" (fly). The red field is 26¼" wide. The red bar is 26¼" wide and the white bar is 26¾" wide. The dates arched above and below the center star are embroidered in white satin stitch.

North Carolina Museum of History, Raleigh, N.C.

47th Regiment
North Carolina State Troops

In September 1863, the regiments of Heth's Division received their new Richmond Depot 3rd bunting issue flags. The following month the regiment was engaged in the Bristoe Campaign and then in November at Mine Run. The following year the 47th Regiment North Carolina State Troops began the spring campaign at the Wilderness and fought in every subsequent campaign associated with the Army of Northern Virginia.

This flag was carried through all the above campaigns. It is 49" (hoist) x 49¾" (fly). The red field is crossed with 5"-wide blue bars, which are edged with ½" white fimbriation. Thirteen 3½" white stars are sewn to the cross at 6" centers. The flag is edged on three sides with 3" white bunting and on the hoist with 1¾" canvas pierced with three whipped eyelets.

According to the War Department records this flag was *"captured at the Battle of Hatcher's Run on October 27, 1864 by Serg't David Murphy, 19th Mass. Vols."* Either the place or date is in error. The 47th was at Burgess' Mill on October 27, and at Hatchers' Run on February 5-7, 1865.

North Carolina Museum of History, Raleigh, N.C.

48th Regiment
North Carolina State Troops

The 48th Regiment North Carolina State Troops was organized on April 9, 1862, around which time the above flag was issued. Attached to Ransom's Brigade in June, the regiment saw action at the Seven Days battles. With Walker's/Cooke's Brigade, the 48th regiment fought at Harpers Ferry and Sharpsburg. Assigned to the Department of South Carolina in the summer of 1863, it returned to Virginia in October, participating in battles at Bristoe and Mine Run. From this point, the regiment served in every subsequent campaign of the Army of Northern Virginia.

The state flag of the 48th Regiment is 54" (hoist) x 80¾" (fly). The red field is 26¾" and is centered with an appliqued 19⅜"-diameter star. The prescribed dates are embroidered in white satin stitch. The individuality of this flag lies in the method of displaying battle honors. On the obverse, twenty remain, each printed in black Roman uncials on 1¼" x 9⅛" white cotton ribbon and sewn at 40-degree angles from the horizontal.

On the obverse, the first row shows honors for FRENCH'S STATION, SHARPSBURG, MINE RUN, HANOVER, and RICHMOND; the second row, HARPER'S FERRY *[sic]*, BRISTOWE *[sic]*, SPOTTSYLVANIA, and REAM'S STATION; the third, FREDERICKSBURG, POE RIVER, FARMVILLE, APPOMATTOX, and HATCHER'S RUN; the fourth, WILDERNESS, GUERLEY'S FARM, and BELLEFIELD; the fifth, COLD HARBOR, SQIRREL *[sic]* LEVEL, and JARRETT'S STATION.

North Carolina Museum of History, Raleigh, N.C.

49th Regiment
North Carolina State Troops

The 49th Regiment North Carolina State Troops was organized on April 12, 1862, at Garysburg, North Carolina. At its formation, the regiment was commanded by the gallant Stephen D. Ramseur. As a part of Ramsom's Brigade, Department of North Carolina, the regiment saw action in the Seven Days battles around Richmond.

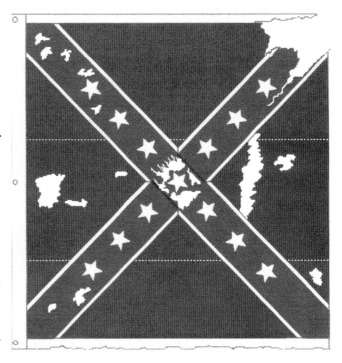

The 49th Regiment remained with Ransom's Brigade throughout the war, seeing service at Harpers Ferry, Sharpsburg, and Fredericksburg.

Before leaving Virginia for duty in North Carolina, the regiment was issued this Army of Northern Virginia battle flag. This Richmond Depot flag was carried through the battles in North Carolina, including Sandy Ridge, Bottom's Bridge, New Berne, and Plymouth.

The regiment returned to Virginia and saw action at Drewry's Bluff, Bermuda Hundred, and the Petersburg Siege. On July 30, 1864, at the Battle of the Crater, this flag was captured by Captain Wright of the 43rd U.S. Colored Troops.

It is a standard 3rd issue flag, 47" (hoist) x 48½" (fly), hand-sewn of wool bunting. The red field is crossed by 5¼"-wide blue bars, which are edged with ½"-wide white cotton fimbriation. Thirteen 3¼" stars are sewn at 6" intervals. The flag is edged on three sides with 2" white bunting. The hoist edge is 2¼" canvas and is pierced with three whipped eyelets.

North Carolina Museum of History, Raleigh, N.C.

49th Regiment
North Carolina State Troops

Because of battlefield losses among Gordon's Corps, hit particularly hard at Cedar Creek, the Richmond Depot produced a sixth version of the bunting battle flag. The 49th Regiment North Carolina State Troops received this flag in early 1865. It is 48½" (hoist) x 47½" (fly). The red field is crossed with 6½"-wide blue bars, which are edged with ¾" white cotton fimbriation. Thirteen 5¼" white stars are sewn to the blue cross at 8" intervals. The flag is edged on three sides with 1½" white bunting and on the hoist with 1¾" canvas heading pierced with three whipped eyelets.

This flag was captured at Five Forks, Virginia, on April 1, 1865, by Lt. Albert E. Fernald, 20th Maine Infantry. It was returned to the War Department and given capture number 281.

Museum of the Confederacy, Richmond, Va.

50th Regiment
North Carolina State Troops

The 50th Regiment North Carolina State Troops was organized at Camp Mangum, near Raleigh, on April 15, 1862. Assigned to Daniel's Brigade, Department of North Carolina, the regiment saw action in the Seven Days battles and at Malvern Hill in Virginia. Returning to North Carolina, the regiment served in the Department of North Carolina/District of the Cape Fear, participating in the Savannah Campaign and the Carolinas Campaign, and surrendered with General Johnston at Durham Station on April 26, 1865.

The flag fragment of the 50th Regiment, approximately 38" square, could be the canton from a 2nd or 3rd National flag. The blue bars are 7½" wide and are bordered with 1"-wide white cotton fimbriation. Thirteen 4½" stars are sewn 7" center to center. These measurements were more common to a battle flag produced by the Department of South Carolina and, due to the regiment's extended service in the Carolinas, it may be that this flag was of Charleston manufacture.

North Carolina Museum of History, Raleigh, N.C.

51st Regiment
North Carolina State Troops

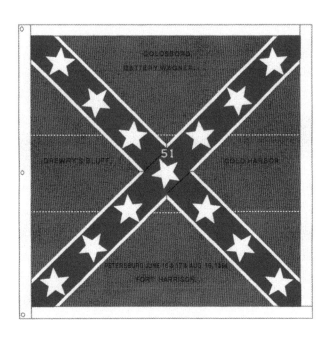

The 51st Regiment North Carolina State Troops was organized at Wilmington on April 13, 1862. For the duration of its service, the regiment was a part of Clingman's Brigade, Department of North Carolina and Southern Virginia/Department of South Carolina, Georgia, and Florida/Department of North Carolina. In addition to the above honors, the regiment saw action in the recapture of Plymouth, North Carolina, on April 17-20, 1864, and at the second assault on Fort Fisher, January 13-15, 1865. The remains of the regiment were surrendered by Gen. Joseph E. Johnston at Durham, on April 26, 1865.

The above flag is a Richmond Depot 4th bunting issue and is one of only two of that issue that displayed honors (the other being that of the 8th North Carolina). It was likely presented to the regiment prior to its return to North Carolina. It is 50" (hoist) x 51" (fly) and is crossed by 5"-wide blue bars, which are edged with ¾"-wide white fimbriation. Thirteen 5"-diameter stars are sewn at 8" intervals. The flag is bordered on three sides with 2"-wide bunting and along the hoist with 2"-wide canvas pierced with three whipped eyelets.

North Carolina Museum of History, Raleigh, N.C.

52nd Regiment
North Carolina State Troops

The 52nd Regiment North Carolina State Troops was organized at Camp Mangum on April 22, 1862. The regiment was first attached to the Department of North Carolina. In September 1862, the regiment was placed under the command of Brigadier General Pettigrew, and served in this capacity through the rest of the war. The 52nd saw its first action at Blackwater River, near Franklin, Virginia, in October 1862. The regiment marched to Gettysburg with Pettigrew's Brigade, Heth's Division, Army of Northern Virginia. They saw action at Falling Waters, Bristoe, and Mine Run. In 1864 and 1865, the regiment participated in every campaign of the Army of Northern Virginia and surrendered at Appomattox.

This flag is 47" (hoist) x 50" (fly). The red field is crossed with 5"-wide blue bars, which are edged with ½" white fimbriation. Thirteen 3½"-diameter stars are spaced on 6" centers. Three sides are edged with 2" white bunting. The hoist edge is 1⅞" canvas pierced with three whipped eyelets.

North Carolina Museum of History, Raleigh, N.C.

Misidentified Flag
(incorrectly identified as 54th N.C.S.T.)

An unidentified battle flag was returned to North Carolina in the general return of 1905. Later it was incorrectly identified as that of the 54th Regiment North Carolina State Troops. The captor's name, "Gaunt," is written on the canvas heading. John C. Gaunt, 104th Ohio Volunteers, captured a flag at Franklin, Tennessee. This flag was forwarded to the War Department.

This flag is similar to the type used by the Department of Alabama and Mississippi, except for its unusual length. It is 45" (hoist) x 62" (fly). The red field is crossed with 7"-wide blue bars, which are edged with 1½" white fimbriation. Twelve 3⅞" cotton stars are sewn to the cross. Along the hoist is a 2" canvas sleeve.

The 54th Regiment North Carolina State Troops was not at Franklin. A flag of the 54th Regiment was captured by Cpl. Theodore Shackelford, Company A, 5th Maine Infantry, at Rappahannock Station, Virginia, on November 7, 1863. It was sent to the War Department and given capture number 6. This flag, however, according to Howard Madaus, has "disappeared."

North Carolina Museum of History, Raleigh, N.C.

55th Regiment
North Carolina State Troops

The 55th Regiment North Carolina State Troops was organized at Camp Mangum in May 1862, with Col. John K. Connally commanding. The regiment was first attached to Samuel G. French's command, Department of North Carolina and Southern Virginia, and saw action in the Suffolk Campaign and at Battery Huger. For most of its service, the 55th Regiment served in Joseph R. Davis' Brigade, Hill's/ Heth's Division.

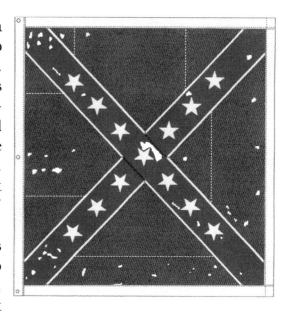

On the morning of July 1, 1863, Heth's Division led the Confederate column to Gettysburg. As attack formation developed, the 55th found itself on the extreme left receiving the first fire from the enemy. Davis' Brigade charged and, as it reached the enemy, wheeled right, enveloping the enemy, who abandoned the position. In the advance, Colonel Connally seized the flag from the fallen color bearer, and waving it high over his head, rushed forward. He was wounded in the hip and arm.

Maj. Alfred Horatio Belo, rushing to the fallen colonel, asked if his wounds were serious. Connally replied in the affirmative, but said, *"Pay no attention to me! Take the colors and keep ahead of the Mississippians."* Belo did so. But as the attacks faltered elsewhere on the field, the 55th found themselves fighting rear guard position for a retreat. The Federals regrouped and the regiment was seriously engaged, firing while falling back.

The handmade bunting flag of the 55th Regiment is 48" (hoist) x 46½" (fly). The red field is crossed by 5"-wide blue bars forming a St. Andrew's cross on which are thirteen 3½" polished cotton stars, spaced 6" apart. The bars are bordered with ½"-wide polished cotton fimbriation. The flag is bordered on three sides by 2" bunting edging and on the hoist with 2"-wide canvas pierced with three whipped eyelets.

The flag was likely captured at Gettysburg and bears capture number 75.

Museum of the Confederacy, Richmond, Va.

55th Regiment
North Carolina State Troops

From July 1863, the 55th Regiment North Carolina State Troops served in Davis'/Cooke's Brigade, Heth's Division, 3rd Corps, Army of Northern Virginia. The regiment saw action during the Bristoe Campaign, Mine Run, Wilderness, Spottsylvania Court House, North Anna, and Cold Harbor and participated in the Petersburg Siege. The above flag was captured during the fight at Weldon Railroad on August 19, 1864, by Pvt. Jennings, Company K, 56th Pennsylvania Volunteers.

The flag is 47½" (hoist) x 46" (fly, remaining). The red field is crossed with 4⅜" blue bars which, are edged with ⅝" white cotton fimbriation. One honor, "GETTYSBURG," is painted in blue block letters in the top quadrant. The unit designation is painted in gold above and below the center star. When new the flag bore thirteen 3⅜" white cotton stars, twelve of which remain with three being fragmentary. Remaining borders are 2⅛" white bunting while the hoist is 1⅝" canvas pierced with three whipped eyelets.

North Carolina Museum of History, Raleigh, N.C.

58th Regiment
North Carolina State Troops

The 58th Regiment North Carolina State Troops, also known as the "58th Partisan Rangers," was organized in Mitchell County on July 24, 1862. The regiment was field consolidated with the 60th Infantry Regiment from December 1863 for the rest of the war. First assigned to the Department of East Tennessee, the regiment saw service in the Army of Tennessee. The regiment saw action at Chickamauga, Chattanooga, the Atlanta Campaign, and Jonesboro. Returning east with General Johnston, the regiment participated in the Carolinas Campaign and fought in the Battle of Bentonville, North Carolina.

The battle flag of the 58th Regiment is fragmentary. There are enough surviving fragments to indicate that the flag was 32" (hoist) x about 38" (fly), an artillery-sized Army of Tennessee issue. The St. Andrew's cross was composed of 5"-wide dark-blue bunting edged with 1⅞"-wide white cotton fimbriation. Thirteen 3"-diameter white cotton stars, or the remnants thereof, remain. The remains of one of the three pairs of ties is sewn to the center of the hemmed edge.

North Carolina Museum of History, Raleigh, N.C.

Beaufort Plow Boys
Co. B, 61st Regiment North Carolina State Troops

This company, known as the "Beaufort Plow Boys," was raised in Beaufort County in October 1861 as Capt. Henry Harding's Independent Company North Carolina Troops. It was mustered into Confederate service at Washington on November 9, 1861, for twelve months. On an unknown date sometime after April 15, 1862, its term of service was extended to three years or the duration of the war.

On or about September 5, 1862, the company was assigned to the newly organized 59th Regiment North Carolina State Troops. That unit was redesignated the 61st Regiment North Carolina State Troops on an unknown date between October 30 and November 22, 1862. This company joined the regiment as Company B, and served with that regiment for the duration of the war.

The flag is a 1st National variant. It is 34½" (hoist) x 70" (fly). The canton is 23" (hoist) x 24" (fly). Thirteen 4"-diameter white stars are sewn to the canton in a radial pattern with one in the center and four in each corner. The unit designation is composed of 4½"-high white bunting block letters, which are backed with paper and appliqued to the obverse. "BEAUFORT" is sewn in an arch to the field's top red bar and "PLOW·BOYS" to the lower. The lower hoist corner is missing a fragment and the upper fly corner is missing considerable material. Other than that, the flag is in good condition.

North Carolina Museum of History, Raleigh, N.C.

61st Regiment
North Carolina State Troops

The 61st Regiment North Carolina State Troops was organized at Wilmington on September 5, 1862. This North Carolina Clothing Depot state flag was issued to the regiment at the time of its formation. As a part of Clingman's Brigade, the regiment saw service in the Department of North Carolina and Southern Virginia, participating in the battle at Grimball's Landing, James Island, South Carolina, Batchelder's Creek, and the recapture of Plymouth, North Carolina, April 17-20, 1864. Transferred to Virginia, the regiment saw action at Drewry's Bluff, Cold Harbor, Petersburg, Globe Tavern, and Fort Harrison. Returning to North Carolina, the 61st took part in the defense of Fort Fisher, January 13-15, 1865, and was surrendered by General Johnston at Durham Station.

The flag is 52" (hoist) x 82⅞" (fly). The red field is 25¾" wide. Centered on the red field is a 17"-diameter white cotton star above and below which are the dates prescribed by the 1861 Flag Act embroidered in white. The unit designation is embroidered along the bottom edge of the red field. The blue and white bars are each 26" wide.

North Carolina Museum of History, Raleigh, N.C.

Brevard Rangers
Co. K, 62nd Regiment North Carolina State Troops

The flag of Company K, 62nd Regiment North Carolina State Troops, is a 1st National variant. It is 36" (hoist) x 51" (fly), including a 1¼" heading to which are attached four sets of 6"-long white cotton ties. The blue canton is 22⅛" (hoist) x 20⅜" (fly). On the obverse side of the canton is the unit name, "BREVARD RANGERS," appliqued in white. On the reverse are twelve six-pointed stars, each one centered with a ¾"-diameter button-like cluster of sequins and gold thread. In the lower corners of the reverse canton are the letters "N" and "C," constructed of ¼"-wide white ribbons.

This flag was captured by Sgt. Cyrus Houch, Company E, 11th Regiment, Michigan Volunteer Cavalry at Asheville. It was returned to North Carolina at a ceremony in Lansing, Michigan on September 20, 1941.

North Carolina Museum of History, Raleigh, N.C.

63rd Regiment North Carolina State Troops

5th Regiment North Carolina Cavalry

The 63rd Regiment North Carolina State Troops was organized by the assignment of the three North Carolina companies of White's (Virginia and North Carolina) Partisan Rangers Battalion, Evans' Partisan Rangers Battalion (five companies), and two independent companies at Camp Long, Garysburg, Northampton County, on September 30, 1862. From its organization until April 1863, the 3rd Regiment North Carolina Cavalry served as a part of the Cavalry Brigade, Department of North Carolina and Southern Virginia. Afterward the regiment became part of Bakers/ Gordon's/Barringer's Brigade, Army of Northern Virginia.

The regiment's engagements with the enemy were numerous; a few notable ones were New Berne, Brandy Station, Culpeper Court House, Manassas Junction, Hanover Court House, Petersburg, and Hampton's Beef Steak Raid.

This flag is a Richmond Depot 3rd (bunting) issue and is 46" (hoist) x 48½" (fly). The red field is crossed with 4¾" blue bars, which are edged with ½" white fimbriation. Thirteen 3⅜"-diameter white cotton stars are spaced 6" apart. The flag is bordered on three sides with 1½" cotton on the hoist with 1⅞" canvas pierced with three whipped eyelets.

North Carolina Museum of History, Raleigh, N.C.

67th Regiment
North Carolina State Troops

This silk 2nd National flag of the 67th Regiment North Carolina State Troops does not conform to government standards and is likely of private manufacture. The 2nd National flag was approved by the Confederate Congress in May 1863, so this flag would have been made after that date. It is 48" (hoist) x 81⅛" (fly). The canton is 28" (hoist) x 26¼" (fly). The St. Andrews cross is constructed of 6"-wide blue bars edged with ½"-wide fimbriation, one bar laid across the other. Thirteen stars 4⅜" in diameter are sewn to the cross. Along the hoist are the remains of seven sets of ties and two eyelets. "Col. J. N. Whitford" is written along the staff edge.

The flag is badly stained and shattered.

North Carolina Museum of History, Raleigh, N.C.

67th Regiment
North Carolina State Troops

The 67th Regiment North Carolina State Troops was organized in state service by the change of designation of the 1st Infantry Battalion, Local Defense Troops, on January 18, 1864. Company K was a cavalry company. Under Col. John N. Whitford, the regiment was attached to the Department of North Carolina and saw action during the Carolinas Campaign in the spring of 1865. The regiment was surrendered at Durham Station on April 26, 1865.

This flag is 46" (hoist) x 46" (fly). The red bunting field is crossed by 4⅝"-4¾"-wide blue bars bordered with ⅞"-wide white cotton fimbriation. Thirteen 3⅜"-diameter white stars are spaced at 6" centers on the St. Andrew's Cross. Three edges are bordered with 2"-wide white bunting. The hoist is bordered with 2"-wide canvas and is pierced with five evenly spaced grommets (probably a post-war addition).

North Carolina Museum of History, Raleigh, N.C.

72nd Regiment North Carolina State Troops

3rd Regiment Junior Reserves

At the battles of Averasboro and Bentonville, a gallant band of boys formed the largest brigade in the skeleton armies with which generals William H. Hardee and Joseph E. Johnston made the last stand of the war in the east. Every member in the ranks was under 18 years old. Nearly every line officer was under 18. They were termed by Governor Vance, the *"seed corn of the Confederacy."* It was glory mixed with anguish to see the beardless boys marching eagerly from their home to serve their state.

The formation of these regiments sprang from the change in the Conscription Act allowing recruitment of soldiers of ages 17 to 50. Governor Vance chose not to mix the youth and the veterans. Instead, he separated them into Junior Reserves and the Senior Reserves. The Junior Reserves, 70th-72nd Regiments North Carolina State Troops, served with honor not only in their home state but also in Virginia under General Hoke.

This remnant is all that is left of the 3rd Regiment Junior Reserves' flag. At its widest point it is about 29⅞". The blue bars are 4" wide and are edged with 1" fimbriation. Five 3½"-diameter stars remain on this fragment of a flag. It appears to have once been a 2nd National flag. It cannot be determined, but what is left of the design is similar to the Sugar Loaf flag of the Senior Reserves.

North Carolina Museum of History, Raleigh, N.C.

3rd National Flag
Sugar Loaf

This flag is the only known example of a 3rd National flag used by North Carolina troops in battle. Although the existence of any 3rd National raises doubts due to its late adoption, this flag's construction is period and the history is reasonable. According to tradition, this flag was used at Sugar Loaf after the Fort Fisher campaigns by John K. Connally's Senior Reserve Brigade, composed of the 73rd-78th Regiments North Carolina State Troops.

It was cared for after the war by George Washington Woodward, a 20-year veteran of the Fayetteville Independent Light Infantry who, though too old for regular service, served in Connally's Brigade. The flag was passed down through his family until acquired by the Cape Fear Museum in 1982.

The flag is 37⅞" (hoist) x 57⅛" (fly). The red canton is 24" square and is crossed with 2¾" blue bars forming a St. Andrew's cross. The cross is edged with ¾"-wide white fimbriation. Thirteen stars are evenly spaced on the cross. The red bar along the fly is 9⅜" wide.

Cape Fear Museum, Wilmington, N.C.

Thomas' Legion

At age 54, William Holland Thomas raised a company of Cherokee soldiers. On April 29, 1862, he was appointed to the rank of captain. He raised a second company and was promoted to major. He actively recruited through the summer and by September 27 his force was a regiment. In the fall, Thomas joined with William Walker to raise a battalion. By June 1863, Thomas' Legion was 2,800 strong, including a company of miners and sappers and a battery of artillery.

Although the mountains have always been a haven for independent-minded and self-sufficient people, they have also been a place of escape for those outside the law. Deserters, using the mountains as a hideout, supported themselves in their self-imposed exile through robbery and thievery. In their role of protector for the mountain people, Thomas' Legion patrolled the valleys and ridges, often apprehending deserters. Other problems arose from "tories" taking advantage of the disorder that accompanies war.

With Union incursions into Tennessee, the Legion was transferred to Strawberry Plain to guard the gaps between Tennessee and Kentucky. The Legion found itself broken up into smaller units, detached to other brigades, and fighting small skirmishes as Union cavalry tested the Confederate defenses. At Telfard's Station, Limestone Station, and Henderson's Mill, the men of Thomas' Legion were a credit to their gray uniforms.

As the unit to which they were attached was withdrawing before the enemy, a regiment of Indiana cavalry began attacking from the rear. Thomas' Legion turned and, in an energetic assault, swept the cavalrymen from the field. Of their action, General Williams said, *"Such exhibition of valor and soldierly bearing will receive, as it deserves, the everlasting remembrance of a grateful country and will ever be an object of pride to their General."*

By November 1864, Thomas' efforts were rewarded, the Legion reunited, and by April 1865 was up to 1,200 men. But while the Legion was growing the Confederacy was fading. By May 1865, the Legion represented the only Confederate resistance in the state. On May 9, Company F of Love's Regiment engaged a portion of the 2nd North Carolina Federal Mounted Infantry under Lt. Col. W. C. Bartlett between Waynesville and Asheville. Bartlett fell back to Waynesville and found himself surrounded by the Cherokee Battalion and Love's Regiment. Bartlett sent word that he wanted a conference.

On the morning of May 10, Brigadier General Martin, overall Confederate commander, Colonel Thomas, and Colonel Love, accompanied by twenty of Thomas' largest braves, attended the conference in Indian regalia. Thomas let it be known that he was attending from a position of strength and suggested that Bartlett and his men may be "scalped" immediately if they did not surrender. Bartlett quickly explained the situation in the rest of the South, adding that should Thomas hold out he could be considered an outlaw and a renegade. Thomas saw the wisdom of capitulation and agreed, but only with the terms that his men return with their arms to their homes and Bartlett leave the area immediately. Bartlett left that day.

The Thomas Legion was the last Confederate force in the east to give up the fight. Ironically, their brothers in the west under Gen. Stand Watie were the last western force to surrender.

The flag of Thomas' Legion is 48" square. The red field is crossed with $4\frac{3}{8}$"-wide blue bars, which are edged with $\frac{3}{4}$" white cotton fimbriation. Thirteen $4\frac{1}{4}$" white cotton stars are sewn to the cross spaced $6\frac{1}{2}$" center to center. The flag is bordered on three sides with $1\frac{1}{2}$" white bunting and on the hoist with $1\frac{3}{4}$" canvas, which is pierced with three whipped eyelets.

Museum of the Cherokee Indian, Cherokee, N.C.

Members of William Holland Thomas' Legion of Indians and Highlanders in attendance at the United Confederate Veterans reunion in New Orleans, 1901.

Front row, left to right: Young Deer, unidentified man, Pheasant, Chief David Reed, Sevier Skitty. Back row, left to right: the Reverend Bird Saloneta, Dickey Driver, Lt. Col. W. W. Stringfield, Lt. Suatie Owl, Jim Keg, Wesley Crow, unidentified man, Lt. Calvin Cagle.

Confederate States Revenue Service

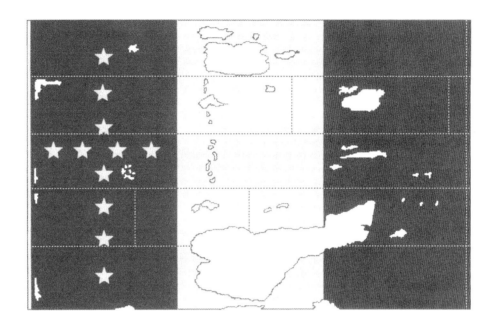

The Confederate States Revenue Service operated in the capacity of the modern-day Coast Guard or possibly as "commercial raiders." This small fleet of ships was overseen by the Department of the Treasury under Secretary C. G. Memminger of South Carolina. It is said that another South Carolinian, Dr. H. D. Capers, chief clerk of the Department of the Treasury, designed the flag of the Revenue Service. Capers' design followed the format of the U.S. Revenue Service in rearranging the 1st National in vertical format and showing only one red bar. A circle of stars was shown on a blue bar that was wider than the others.

The above Revenue Service flag differs slightly from the specified design in that the three bars are of equal width and the stars are displayed in the form of a cross. The flag is 91" (hoist) x 142" (fly). The field is composed of vertical bars that are blue/white/red and are 46½"/48"/47", respectively. The flag is constructed of five horizontal panels that are 18"/18"/18"/18½"/18½", respectively. Eleven 5"-diameter stars are sewn to the blue bar in the form of a Latin cross.

This flag was taken from an unidentified Confederate gunboat at Roanoke Island, North Carolina.

Museum of the Confederacy, Richmond, Va.

C.S.S. *Albemarle*

Criticized by one of its own crewmen as "the poorest ironclad in the Confederacy," the *C.S.S. Albemarle* rose from the humblest of beginnings to become a most feared and formidable adversary for the Federal Navy occupying the sounds of North Carolina. For lack of a shipyard, the ironclad was constructed on a riverbank.

For lack of iron plate, the ship was armored with salvaged iron worked by blacksmiths at portable forges. Loggers from local farms brought in lumber on oxcarts. When a twist bit was needed to bore holes in the iron, a local

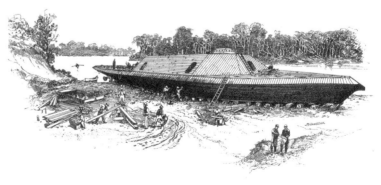

farmer's son invented one. The ironclad was actually still under construction when it left on its first mission, the retaking of Plymouth, North Carolina.

The *C.S.S. Albemarle* steamed downriver and on April 19, 1864, engaged two Union warships, the *U.S.S. Miami* and the *U.S.S. Southfield*, sent to prevent her from carrying out her mission. Deftly avoiding a trap laid by the two ships, Cmdr. James W. Cooke steered his ram straight for the pair of ships. Glancing off the *Miami*, Cooke (right) sent the iron prow of the *Albemarle* crashing into the *Southfield*, opening a gaping hole in the side of the Union ship and sending it straight to the river's bottom. The *Miami*'s commander was killed when a cannon round he fired at the Confederate ironclad ricocheted off the ship's armor and exploded, killing him instantly and wounding a number of his gun crew. The *Miami* retreated, and the *Albemarle* continued on its mission to Plymouth.

As the *Albemarle* cleared the river of Union ships and engaged the Federal shore batteries at Plymouth, Gen. Robert Hoke attacked from the land. At 10 A.M., the occupying Union forces accepted terms from General Hoke. The joint army-navy assault was a great success and was a source of tremendous encouragement for Confederate hopes in the sounds of North Carolina. Fearing the loss of this important area, the Union authorities began to make plans for the ram's demise.

This flag of the *Albemarle* was taken by Sailing Master George F. Ford, U.S.N., in October 1864 when the *Albemarle* was sunk. It is 80" (hoist) x 125" (fly). The canton is 50" (hoist) x 55" (fly). The red field is crossed with 9½" blue bars forming a St. Andrew's cross, which is edged with 1½" white cotton fimbriation. The white bunting field of this 2nd National flag is composed of five panels, 16"-18" wide, with a 1¼" supplementary strip at the top. Along the hoist is a 1½"-wide canvas sleeve through which a rope was passed.

Museum of the Confederacy, Richmond, Va.

C.S.S. *Albemarle*

Recently promoted for his success at Plymouth, Maj. Gen. Robert Hoke began making plans to recapture Washington, North Carolina. But on April 30 the town was abandoned. The Federals, unable to hold the town on the shore of Albemarle Sound, evacuated by ship, but not before looting and setting fires. The blaze destroyed over half the town.

Enraged, Hoke determined to drive the Federals from the shores of his state. Plans were made to take New Berne, and the *Albemarle* would be crucial to these plans. Cooke agreed and pledged his cooperation although the *Albemarle* would have to cross Albemarle Sound and engage not two ships but the Union fleet. On May 5, the *Albemarle* left her mooring and sailed for the open sound. She was met at the mouth of the sound by seven Union warships. Four of these, the *Mattabesset, Sassacus, Wyalusing,* and *Miami,* were large double-ended warships armed with 9-inch Dahlgrens and 100-pounder Parrotts. With the three smaller gunboats, *Ceres, Whitehead,* and *Commodore Hull,* the Union armament was fifty-eight guns.

Nevertheless, Cooke sailed straight for the fleet with his forward gun opening the battle. The first shots struck the *Mattabessett,* taking away the railing around her pivot-rifle and wounding six gunners. The *Sassacus* then engaged with a broadside of 9" rounds that bounced harmlessly off the side of the *Albemarle.* Stoking his furnaces with oil-soaked rags, the commander of the *Sassacus* circled and, with a full head of steam, crashed his ship into the side of the ironclad. The bow of the *Sassacus* was demolished by the blow, and the ship began drifting broadside to the ironclad. Seconds later a shot was fired from the *Albemarle's* Brooke rifle that holed the Union double-ender and pierced its boiler, sending super-saturated steam rushing through the engine room horribly scalding the hapless sailors.

The battle had been engaged at 4:40 P.M. The *Sassascus* played her final card by ramming the ironclad at 5:05. In these fifteen minutes, the

Mattabessett was damaged with many wounded; the *Sassacus* was crippled with many killed; the *Wyalusing* had been struck so badly that the commander signaled that he was sinking; the *Miami*, even though armed with a spar torpedo, did not engage, and the three smaller ships wisely sat off at a distance and watched the battle.

The battered fleet retired from the field, but the *Albemarle*, too, had taken its share of hits. The smokestack was perforated with shot (right) prohibiting proper operation of the engines. The rudder had been damaged in the fight. Too disabled to be effective in the New Berne operation, the ship returned up the Roanoke and anchored off Plymouth.

Desperate to remove the Albemarle as a factor in the sounds of North Carolina, the Federal government offered a reward to anyone who could take out the formidable ironclad. On the night of October 27, 1864, a clandestine mission led by Lt. William B. Cushing moved up the Roanoke in a torpedo launch. The quiet-running craft allowed the raiders to get within attacking distance before they were detected. In a rush forward, Cushing placed the spar-torpedo and pulled the pin just as the gunners of the *Albemarle* fired their first shot. The torpedo boat was swamped by the blast. The hole opened in the lower hull of the ironclad proved fatal and gave the ship the dubious distinction of being the only Confederate ironclad sunk by enemy action.

This flag of the *C.S.S. Albemarle* was captured after the action of October 27, 1864. It is 105" (hoist) x 200" (fly, remaining). The canton is 68" (hoist) x 66" (fly) and is crossed with 12"-wide blue bars edged with 3" white fimbriation. Thirteen 10"-diameter stars are sewn to the cross at 12"-14" intervals. The white field is composed of six panels 16½"-18" wide. Along the hoist is a 2½"-wide canvas heading, which is reinforced top and bottom with 8"-long strips of canvas.

Museum of the Confederacy, Richmond, Va.

C.S.S. *Shenandoah*

From October 1864 to June 1865, the Confederate sloop *Shenandoah* circumnavigated the globe, destroying thirty-nine Federal merchant ships and whalers and devastating the United States whaling industry. The cruiser's most stellar successes occurred in the Bering Sea. North Carolinian Captain James Iredell Waddell (below), commander of the *Shenandoah,* learned of the war's end only in late June from a British ship. Rather than surrender to Union authorities, Waddell sailed to England and surrendered to the British on November 6, 1865.

This flag of the *Shenandoah* is constructed in British configuration, the rectangular canton representing roughly one-fourth of the field. It is 88" (hoist) x 136" (fly), which gives the flag a 4:6 ratio. The canton is 44" (hoist) x 58½" (fly). Blue bars, 3" wide and edged with 1"-wide fimbriation, form a St. Andrew's cross. Thirteen 2¾"-diameter gold stars are painted to the cross. Lt. Dabney Scales gave this flag to his cousin for safekeeping. In 1873, the flag was brought to the United States from England, and it was donated to the Museum of the Confederacy in 1907.

Museum of the Confederacy, Richmond, Va.

Blockade Runner
(Unidentified)

On April 16, 1861, President Lincoln proclaimed a blockade of the Southern coast including the coast of North Carolina, a state that, at that time, was struggling to remain in the Union. Although the news had an unsettling effect, it would be over a month before the Old North State would separate itself from the Union.

The port of Wilmington became one of the most important ports for the Confederacy, and the railroad leaving Wilmington for Virginia, the Wilmington and Weldon, became famous as the "lifeline of the Confederacy." Blockade Runners, sleek, fast steamers painted matte gray, raced in and out of Wilmington through the fleet of Union blockaders. Through the war, over 300 of these ships arrived at North Carolina ports with supplies vital to the life of the South and left bearing with them cotton and other export goods for the world. The fall of Fort Fisher in February 1865 closed the port of Wilmington and signaled the death knell of the Confederacy.

This flag was taken from a blockade runner in Wilmington after its capture by Union forces. It is 101½" (hoist) x 162" (fly, remaining). The canton is 71" (hoist) x 77½" (fly). The red field is crossed with 8½"-wide blue bunting bars edged with 2½" white fimbriation. Thirteen 6"-diameter white stars are sewn to the cross at 12" intervals. Along the hoist is a 3" canvas sleeve. The field is constructed of white bunting panels that vary in width from 16½" to 17¼".

Museum of the Confederacy, Richmond, Va.

North Carolina Flags Not Shown

North Carolina History Museum

1. 3rd Regt. N.C.S.T.; state flag, 1914.256.1

   State flag; 35"; unit designation on obverse; dates on reverse; presented to Governor Vance after the battle of Sharpsburg. This flag is of similar construction to those of the 2nd and 8th Regiments.

2. 4th Regt. N.C.S.T.; anv; 1952.26.1
   A miniature (14") made from the remains of a silk battle flag that was presented to Major Myers by ladies of Rowan County; 13 stars embroidered in satin stitch. The original was probably of 1st (silk) issue construction.

3. North Carolina Grays, Co. I, 6th Regt. N.C.S.T.; 19XX.330.174
   Blue field, white canton with N.C. State seal and "The Old North State Forever"; reverse reads "North Carolina Grays, Presented by Ladies of Cedar Fork." Paint badly cracked; silk fractured.

4. 11th Regt. N.C.S.T.; remnants; 1919.29.1
   At the surrender, officers chose to burn the regimental flag; this small flag was made from three saved remnants.

5. 18th Regt. N.C.S.T.; anv
   Battle flag captured near Petersburg, Apr. 2, 1865; honors in blue

6. 40th Regt. N.C.S.T.; aot
   Army of Tennessee battle flag captured at Bentonville and attributed by its captors to the 40th N.C.S.T.; doubtful since the 40th never served with the AOT

7. 54th Regt. N.C.S.T., WD6, 1927.5.1.
   This flag is "missing."

8. 61st Regt. N.C.S.T.; L.1999.10.4
   No history; a recent acquisition

9. 67th Regt. N.C.S.T., 1916.52.1
   Battle flag

10. 69th Regt. N.C.S.T., 1916.53.1
    Battle flag; no longer with museum; returned to donor, 1964

11. Perquimans Rangers; 1914.383.1
Museum records identify the flag as a Confederate 2nd Nat'l (obverse); N.C. State seal (reverse); 56"; silk; "brittle & shattered"; made by the Ladies of Hertford, N.C., June 1861, and presented to the Perquimans Rangers. Either the pattern or date of production is an error.

12. Fort Macon, 1st Nat'l; 1979.161.1
Confederate 1st Nat'l; 108"; 7 appliqued stars in canton; canvas sleeve with rope

13. North Carolina Defenders, Co. D, 37th Regt. N.C.S.T.; state flag variant, 1916.79.1
Variation of N.C. state flag; gold bar over blue; black 5-pointed star w/40 rays; gold-painted inscription; shattered; paint deteriorated

14. Fayetteville Arsenal, fragment, 1916.24.3
This flag is "missing."

Museum of the Confederacy

1. 1st Regt. N.C.S.T., WD421
Battle flag; 48" x 48"; eight stars remain; honors in blue; captured during Appomattox campaign

2. 12th Regt. N.C.S.T., WD333
Battle flag; 46" x 47"; captured Sayler's Creek, Va., Apr. 1865

3. 33rd Regt. N.C.S.T., WD433
Battle flag; 48½" x 41" (fly end tattered); white honors; captured during Appomattox campaign

4. 47th Regt. N.C.S.T., WD68
Battle flag; 48" x 49"; captured Gettysburg

5. Ransom's Brigade (unidentified), WD278
Battle flag; 46½" x 46"; twelve stars remain; captured Five Forks, Va., Apr. 1865

6. Cox's Brigade (unidentified), WD280
Battle flag; 49" x 49"; two stars remain; honors in blue; captured Appomattox

7. Cooke's Brigade (unidentified), WD52
Battle flag; 45" x 50"; captured Bristoe Station, Va.

8. Cooke's Brigade (unidentified), WD53
Battle flag; 45" x 48"; captured Bristoe Station, Va.

Appendix I
North Carolina State Troops

On April 17, 1861, Governor Ellis, anticipating the likelihood of North Carolina's secession, issued a call for volunteers. The first camp at Raleigh came under the command of D. H. Hill and was designated 1st Regiment Volunteers. A total of fourteen regiments soon volunteered for service. Due to confusion in the organization of the 9th Infantry Volunteers, the regiment was never formed and the 9th designation was assigned to Spruill's cavalry legion.

Coincidental with the formation of these fourteen regiments, ten other regiments were formed and designated "State Troops," regiments 1st - 8th being infantry, the 9th as cavalry, and the 10th as artillery.

The 10th Regiment North Carolina Artillery was composed of ten companies, the first five light artillery and the last five heavy, or coastal, artillery. Because of their diversity of service, the artillery companies did not serve as a regiment but as separate detachments. For this reason they are listed separately below:

Co. A - S.D. Ramseur/Basil Manly
Co. B - James Reilly/John Ramsey;
    "Rowan Artillery"
Co. C - Graham/Williams;
    "Charlotte Artillery"
Co. D - A.D. Moore

Co. E - T.J. Southerland
Co. F - H.T. Guion
Co. G - W.S.G. Andrews
Co. H - J.L. Manney
Co. I - S.D. Pool
Co. K - Thomas K. Sparrow

In this arrangement there was a 1st North Carolina Volunteers and a 1st North Carolina State Troops, a 2nd North Carolina Volunteers, and a 2nd North Carolina State Troops, etc. Due to the confusion caused by this double numbering, the first fourteen regiments of volunteers were redesignated by adding ten to their unit number. Thus the 1st North Carolina Volunteers became the 11th North Carolina State Troops, etc. More regiments followed and by January 1862 North Carolina had fielded forty-one regiments.

Each of North Carolina's regiments was assigned a State Troops designation although the Cavalry and Artillery regiments were secondarily designated by their individual unit number. The final designation of **North Carolina State Troops** is as follows:

1st - 8th	Infantry Regiments	42nd - 58th	Infantry Regiments
9th	1st Cavalry Regiment	59th	4th Cavalry Regiment
10th	1st Artillery Regiment	60th - 62nd	Infantry Regiments
11th - 18th	Infantry Regiments (formerly 1st-8th N.C. Volunteers)	63rd	5th Cavalry Regiment
		64th	Infantry Regiment
		65th	6th Cavalry Regiment
19th	2nd Cavalry Regiment (formerly 9th N.C. Volunteers)	66th - 68th	Infantry Regiments
		69th	7th Cavalry Regiment
		70th - 72nd	1st-3rd Regiments Junior Reserves
20th - 24th	Infantry Regiments (formerly 10th-14th N.C. Volunteers)	73rd - 74th	4th-5th Regiments Senior Reserves
25th - 35th	Infantry Regiments	75th	16th Cavalry Battalion
36th	2nd Artillery Regiment	76th - 78th	6th-8th Regiments Senior Reserves
37th - 39th	Infantry Regiments		
40th	3rd Artillery Regiment		
41st	3rd Cavalry Regiment		

Appendix II

Distribution of North Carolina Regiments in the summer of 1863

Army of Northern Virginia (Gettysburg)
1st Army Corps, Lt. Gen. James Longstreet
    McLaw's Division
        Cabell's Artillery Battalion
            Manly's Battery, Co. A, 1st N.C. Artillery
Hood's Division
    Henry's Artillery Battalion
        Branch (N.C.) Artillery
            Rowan (N.C.) Artillery, Co. D, 1st N.C. Artillery
2nd Army Corps, Lt. Gen. Richard Ewell
    Early's Division
        Hoke's Brigade (Col. Isaac E. Avery)
            6th, 21st, 57th N.C. Regiments, 1st Bn. N.C. Sharpshooters
    Johnson's Division
        Steuart's Brigade (Brig. Gen. George H. Steuart)
            1st, 3rd N.C. Regiments
    Rodes' Division
        Daniel's Brigade (Brig. Gen. Julius Daniel)
            32nd, 43rd, 45th, and 53rd N.C. Regiments
        Iverson's Brigade (Brig. Gen. Alfred Iverson)
            5th, 12th, 20thand 23rd N.C. Regiments
        Ramseur's Brigade (Brig. Gen. S.D. Ramseur)
            2nd, 3rd, 4th, 14th, and 30th N.C. Regiments
3rd Army Corps, Lt. Gen. A.P. Hill
    Heth's Division
        1st Brigade (Brig. Gen. J.J. Pettigrew)
            11th N.C. (band), 26th, 47th, and 52nd N.C. Regiments
        4th Brigade (Brig. Gen. Joseph R. Davis)
            55th N.C. Regiment
    Pender's Division
        2nd Brigade (Brig. Gen. James H. Lane)
            7th, 18th, 28th, 33rd, and 37th N.C. Regiments

4th Brigade (Brig. Gen. A.M. Scales)
    13th (B), 16th, 22nd, 34th and 38th N.C. Regiments
Poague's Artillery Battalion
    Charlotte (N.C.) Artillery
Cavalry
Stuart's Division
  Hampton's Brigade (Brig. Gen. Wade Hampton)
    1st N.C. Cavalry Regiment
  Robertson's Brigade (Brig. Gen. Beverly H. Robertson)
    4th and 5th N.C. Cavalry Regiments
  W. H. F. Lee's Brigade (Col. J.R. Chambliss)
    2nd N.C. Cavalry Regiment

Department of North Carolina

Clingman's Brigade
  8th & 31st N.C. Regiments (at Battery Wagner, S.C.)
  61st N.C. Regiment (battles near Grimball's Landing, James Island, S.C.)
Martin's Brigade
  50th N.C. Regiment
District of North Carolina
  42nd & 66th N.C. Regiments
  12th Battalion N.C. Cavalry
  Swindall's Cavalry Co., Partisan Rangers
Unattached
  54th & 57th N.C. Regiments
Department of South Carolina, Georgia, and Florida
  1st Military District
  51st N.C. Regiment

Department of Richmond

Cooke's Brigade (at S. Anna Bridge)
  15th, 27th, 44th, 46th, & 48th N.C. Regiments
Ransom's Brigade (at Bottom's Bridge)
  24th, 25th, 35th, 49th, & 56th N.C. Regiments

Department of Tennessee

Army of East Tennessee
  Frazer's Brigade
    58th & 64th N.C. Regiments
Gracie's Brigade

62nd N.C. Regiment
Scott's Cavalry Brigade
 5th Battalion N.C. Cavalry
Pegram's Cavalry Brigade
 7th Battalion N.C. Cavalry

Department of Mississippi & E. Louisiana

Walker's Division
Wilson's Brigade
 29th N.C. Regiment

Department of the West

French's Division
McNair's Brigade
 39th N.C. Regiment

Appendix III

The charge of the 26th Regiment North Carolina State Troops at the battle of Gettysburg on July 1, 1863, particularly the casualties taken surrounding the regimental colors.

"All to a man were at once up and ready, every officer at his post, Colonel Burgwyn in the center, Lieutenant Colonel Lane on the right, Major Jones on the left. Our gallant standard-bearer, J.B. Mansfield, at once stepped to his position-four paces to the front, and the eight color guards to their proper places. At the command 'Forward, march!' all to a man stepped off, apparently as willingly and as proudly as if they were on review."

Twenty-sixth Regiment, Clark's Rosters

1. Color Sergeant Jefferson B. Mansfield (wounded)
2. Sgt. Hiram Johnson (wounded)
3. John Stamper (wounded)
4. G. W. Kelly (leg broken by a piece of shell)
5. Lewis A. Thomas, Co. F (wounded)
6. John Vinson, Co. G (wounded)
7. John R. Marley, Co. G (Killed)
8. Unknown soldier (shot down)
9. Unknown soldier (shot down

(At this point, various regimental histories and reminiscences relate that the entire color guard was killed or wounded.)

10. Capt. William Westwood McCreery, General Pettigrew's staff (shot through the heart)
11. Lt. George Wilcox, Co. H (two wounds)
12. Col. "Harry" Burgwyn (killed, after relinquishing the colors to Private Honneycut)
13. Pvt. Franklin L. Honneycut, Co. B (killed)
14. Lt. Col. John Lane (wounded)

Appreciation

There are a few people who have been of help to me who probably do not even remember it. I appreciate the time spent with me and the information shared. The unselfish courtesy that they afforded me over a telephone or in an e-mail is common behavior to North Carolina Southrons.

A heartfelt thank you goes to the many members of the North Carolina Division Sons of Confederate Veterans for their help and encouragement on this work. My appreciation goes also to museum flag curators Ken Blankenship, Chris Graham, and Timothy Bottoms, who shared their valuable time with me. Special thanks to Rebecca Ansel Rose, flag curator at the Museum of the Confederacy, Richmond, Virginia, who, in addition to managing the largest collection of Confederate flags in the world, shared her time, allowing me to examine a group of flags that added greatly to this work.

Heartfelt appreciation goes to my wife, Donna, for her patience and encouragement, for proofreading and sharing ideas, to my son, George, whose creativity, artistry, and help added many finishing touches, and to my son, Reuben, for his cheerful faith and encouragement.

Grateful appreciation to my publisher, Dr. Milburn Calhoun, Pelican Publishing Company, and to my editor, Nina Kooij, who despite my numerous missed deadlines believed in this work and was a constant source of encouragement, assistance, and focus.

A special note of gratitude goes to artist Rick Reeves of Tampa, Florida, for the use of his excellent painting of the 14th Regiment North Carolina Troops for the cover of this book.

Special thanks go to the following individuals:

Tom Belton, Curator of Military History, North Carolina Museum of History; Barry Bingham, Jr., Louisville, Ky.; Ken Blankenship, Museum of the Cherokee Indian, Cherokee, N.C.; Eric Blevins, Photographer, North Carolina Museum of History; Timothy S. Bottoms, Cape Fear Museum, Wilmington, N.C.; George W. Cooper, S.C.V., Asheville, N.C.; Anne E. Douglas, Louisville, Ky.; Glenn N. Fields, S.C.V., Goldsboro, N.C.; Chris Graham, Assistant Curator, North Carolina Museum of History; Edward Harding, S.C.V., Washington, N.C.; Sheri Heavner, Gaston County Museum of History, Dallas, N.C.; James J. Holmberg, Filson Historical Society, Louisville, Ky.; Bob Jones, S.C.V., Florence, S.C.; Roger McCredie, S.C.V., Asheville, N.C.; George

Patterson, S.C.V., Concord, N.C.; Heath F. Ritchie, S.C.V., Concord, N.C.; Rebecca A. Rose, Flag Curator, The Museum of the Confederacy, Richmond, Va.; David Souther, S.C.V., Concord, N.C.; Dr. Mark Wetherington, Filson Historical Society, Louisville, KY; Bernie Thuersam, Board Chairman, Cape Fear Museum, Wilmington, N.C.; Robert Hancock, Curator, Museum of the Confederacy, Richmond V.A.; Sue Miller, Assistant Registrar, Cape Fear Museum, Wilmington, N.C.

Bibliography

Allen, T. Harrell, *Lee's Last Major General: Bryan Grimes of North Carolina.* Mason City, Iowa: Savas Publishing Co., 1999.

Cannon, Devereaux, Jr., *Flags of the Confederacy.* Gretna: Pelican Publishing Co., 1977.

Clark, Walter, ed. *Histories of the Several Regiments and Battalions from North Carolina in the Great War 1861-'65. Written by Members of the Respective Companies.* Goldsboro: Nash Brothers Book and Job Printers, 1901. (These five volumes are usually referred to as "Clark's Rosters.")

Crow, Vernon H., *Storm in the Mountains: Thomas' Confederate Legion of Cherokee Indians and Mountaineers.* Cherokee: Press of the Museum of the Cherokee Indian, 1982.

Crute, Joseph H., Jr., *Emblems of Southern Valor: The Battle Flags of the Confederacy.* Louisville: Harmony House, 1990.

Elliott, Robert G., *Ironclad of the Roanoke: Gilbert Elliott's Albemarle.* Shippensburg: White Mane Publishing Co., 1994.

Flowers, George W., Lt. Col. *The Thirty-Eighth N.C. Regiment. Its History in the Civil War.* Southern Historical Society Papers, Vol. XXV, Jan-Dec. 1897, pp. 245-63.

Gragg, Rod, *The Illustrated Confederate Reader.* New York: Harper & Row, 1989.

Grissom, Michael A., *Southern by the Grace of God.* Gretna: Pelican Publishing Co., 1990.

Harper, George Washington Finley, *Sketch of the Fifty-eighth Regiment (Infantry) North Carolina Troops.*

Hill, D. H., Jr., *Confederate Military History: North Carolina.* Atlanta: Confederate Publishing Co., 1899.

Katcher, Scollins, Embleton, *Flags of the American Civil War 1: Confederate, Men-at-Arms Series, No. 252.* London: Osprey Publishing, Ltd., 1992.

Kennedy, James R.; Kennedy, Walter D., *The South Was Right!* Gretna: Pelican Publishing Co., 1994.

Lefler, Hugh Talmadge; Newsome, Albert Ray, *North Carolina: The History of a Southern State.* Chapel Hill: University of North Carolina Press, 1976 (3rd edition).

McMahon, Thomas L., "The flag of the 5th North Carolina, the first Southern banner captured in the East, has been rediscovered." *America's Civil War,* May 2002: p. 66.

Madaus, Howard Michael, *The Battle Flags of the Confederate Army of Tennessee.* Milwaukee: Milwaukee Public Museum, 1976.

Manarin, Louis H., *North Carolina Troops 1861-1865, A Roster.* Raleigh: North Carolina State Department of Archives and History (multi-volume set, Vol. I, 1996-Vol XIV, 1998).

Mast, Greg, *State Troops and Volunteers—A Photographic Record of North Carolina's Civil War Soldiers.* Raleigh: North Carolina Department of Cultural Resources, Division of Archives and History, 1995.

Medley, Mary L., *History of Anson County, North Carolina 1750-1976.* Baltimore: Clearfield Co., 1993.

Petty, C. Q., Maj., *History of the 49th N.C. Regiment* (an account written "from the records of our Regiment so far as I could get them—the balance from memory and is as nearly correct as I can make it"), July 16, 1894.

Rose, Rebecca Ansel, *Colours of the Gray: An Illustrated Index of Wartime Flags From the Museum of the Confederacy's Collection.* Richmond: 1998.

Schroeder, Patrick A., ed., *Five Points in the Record of North Carolina in the Great War of 1861-5.* Raleigh: North Carolina Literary and Historical Society, 1904 (with new introduction and material by P. A. Schroeder, 2000).

Sifakis, Stewart, *Compendium of the Confederate Armies: North Carolina.* New York: Facts-on-File, 1992.

Sondley, F. A., *A History of Buncombe County, North Carolina.*, Spartanburg: The Reprint Co., 1977 [reprinted from the 1930 edition].

Southern Historical Society Papers, Vol. XXV, Jan-Dec 1897: "The Forty-fourth N.C. Infantry," pp. 334-45.

Summers, T. O., ed., *The Confederate States Almanac For the Year of Our Lord 1862.* Nashville: Southern Methodist Publishing House, 1862.

Taylor, Michael W., *The Cry is War, War, War: The Civil War Correspondence of Lts. Burwell Thomas Cotton and George Job Huntley, 34th Regiment North Carolina Troops.* Dayton, Ohio: Morningside House, 1994.

Tucker, Glenn, *Zeb Vance: Champion of Personal Freedom.* New York: Bobbs-Merrill, 1965.

Wall, H. C., *Historical Sketch of the Pee Dee Guards (Co. D, 23rd N.C. Regiment) from 1861 to 1865.* Raleigh: Edwards, Broughton, & Co., Printers and Binders, 1876.

Wise, Stephen R., *Lifeline of the Confederacy: Blockade Running During the Civil War.* Columbia: University of South Carolina Press, 1988.

Woodhead, Henry, ed., *Echoes of Glory: Arms and Equipment of the Confederacy.* New York: Time-Life, 1991.

Index